ROBERT EXON

ROBERT EXON:

(A Biography of Dr. R.C. Mortimer, Bishop of Exeter from 1949-1973)

B.G. Skinner.

With a Foreword by the Rt. Rev. and Rt. Hon. Lord Ramsey of Canterbury.

Rev. B.G. Skinner

Robert Exon

NEW HORIZON

ISBN 0 86116 136 X

92
M844s

8201181

Copyright © 1979
Rev. B. G. Skinner

New Horizon
Horizon House
5 Victoria Drive
Bognor Regis, Sussex.

TABLE OF CONTENTS

FOREWORD	by the Rt. Rev. and Rt. Hon Lord Ramsey of Canterbury	
PREFACE		
CHAPTER I	Early Days	Page 1
CHAPTER II	To Country Pastures New	6
CHAPTER III	College Days - From Keble to Wells	15
CHAPTER IV	Ordination - and the Parish Round	27
CHAPTER V	The Pinnacle of Christ Church	37
CHAPTER VI	The Later Years at Oxford	48
CHAPTER VII	Consecration and Enthronement	62
CHAPTER VIII	Bishop and Pastor	72
CHAPTER IX	Robert Mortimer - The Man	85
CHAPTER X	The Diocese - Officers and Organisations	96
CHAPTER XI	Notable Events while Bishop of Exeter	110
CHAPTER XII	The Bishop on Convocation and Church Assembly	122
CHAPTER XIII	The House of Lords - and Government Committees	136
CHAPTER XIV	The Bishop's Special Church Interests	145
CHAPTER XV	The World of Education	154
CHAPTER XVI	The Bishop's Later Writings	163
CHAPTER XVII	Eventide Years	170
Memorial Service Address by Professor G.R. Dunstan		184

FOREWORD

by Bishop Michael Ramsey

Robert Mortimer was, in every sense of the word, an outstanding figure among the bishops of his time, and this memoir by one who knew him well gives a vivid picture of him in the setting of the diocese of Exeter, where the Devon people knew his gifts and personality. They were very proud of him, and remember him with gratitude.

I knew him myself in the setting of the central life of the church, and realised how wide was the influence of his wisdom and integrity. He was a statesman, a scholar and a divine, and these three gifts were wonderfully blended: his grasp of relations between church and state, his store of theological and legal knowledge and his devotion to the Lord of the church. He was also a very kind person, and he would bring all his powers to help someone when his help was needed.

A first-rate speaker, lucid, persuasive and humorous, he was listened to with eager attention in Convocation, the Church Assembly and the General Synod. In the House of Lords I do not know of a bishop of the time who was more respected for himself and his speeches. He was felt to speak with authority especially on questions concerning marriage, church legislation, the treatment of crime and the reform of prisons.

Bishop Mortimer was a strong catholic churchman, traditional in training and outlook and very critical of superficial modernity. But his integrity of mind would lead him sometimes into independent and unpredictable positions. His mind was of a finely judicial cast, and it was fascinating to watch his mind at work, sifting the arguments, exposing the fallacies and reaching the conclusion; and it was the same whether he was advising an assembly or helping an individual with a difficult question when his true sympathy as well as his mental power was so apparent.

His friends can never forget the fun of his companionship, and the obvious happiness which he had in his own home and family. I thank God that I had him as a colleague for so many years, and that the Church of England had him just when it did. I am sure that this book will have many grateful readers who will enjoy the story of a most unusual person and will learn much about the Church of England in the last few decades.

    Michael Ramsey

PREFACE

In 1974, when I was Vicar of Brixham, Dr. Mortimer kindly agreed to my writing his biography. Like the Bishop's father I was born at Sidmouth, where my parents lived for fifty years. Although I worked far from Devon for much of the time, we had holidays in the county almost every year, so I watched the whole of Dr. Mortimer's episcopate from a middle distance with great admiration and interest. On the Bishop's death Mrs. Mortimer kindly gave me every assistance and allowed me to see her husband's personal papers.

My greatest difficulty has been to do justice to Dr. Mortimer's vast range of activities in a relatively brief work. One could easily have written a volume of equal length on Dr. Mortimer's contributions to scholarship alone. Another could have been written on his work for Convocation, a third on his work as a Parliamentarian, yet another on his life in the Diocese and certainly another on the Bishop's fascinating character, so beloved of those who knew him well. Where might it have ended? In compressing so much material into one slender volume my aim has been first to paint a portrait of the Bishop as his friends will always remember him and secondly to do some justice to the immense output of his brilliant mind over the years. If in outlining so many and varied activities I have cut the descriptions too short, I can only apologise.

It remains for me to thank those who have been so generous in their help. Apart from Mrs Mortimer, Miss Fookes, and other members of the family, Lord Blake, Sir Hugh Trevor-Roper, the late Sir John Masterman and the Warden of St. Edward's Oxford (Mr. C.H. Christie) very kindly gave me personal interviews. Many more, including the Bishop of Chichester, Bishop R.R. Williams, Sir John Guillum Scott, the Dean of Christ Church, the Warden of Keble and the Rev. Sir Patrick Ferguson-Davie kindly helped me with written contributions. The Rev. G.F. Hilder, formerly Prolocutor of the Lower House of Canterbury Convocation, lent me a long run of the Chronicle of Canterbury Convocation and helped in other ways.

Needless to say, so many clergy and laymen of Exeter Diocese assisted me that it would be impossible to mention all their names. However, I would particularly like to thank Bishop Westall, Archdeacons A.F. Ward and R.J.D. Newhouse and above all *Canon F.G. Rice who was of very great assistance and who perhaps knew the Bishop better than anyone else outside his family. Professor J.R. Porter has given me valuable advice at every stage.

Mr. J.R. Pike, the Torbay Borough Librarian, has been of great assistance, and his colleagues at Torquay Reference Library went to immense pains in bringing up countless newspapers from the stack. I have also been helped by the Bodleian Library, Exeter University and City Libraries and Dr. Williams' Library. Miss K.J. Le Clair, until recently Exeter Diocesan Secretary, kindly gave me access to bound volumes of the *Exeter Diocesan Leaflet*.

Many have paid tribute to Professor G.R. Dunstan's moving address given at the Memorial Service for Dr. Mortimer at Christ Church Cathedral, and I have pleasure in including it with his kind permission. Finally my warmest thanks are due to Bishop Michael Ramsey for most generously giving of his time to write the Foreword to the book.

B.G. Skinner,
Paignton, July, 1978.

*To our great sorrow Canon Rice, who had read the final manuscript and was much looking forward to seeing the book, died in December 1978.

ROBERT MORTIMER AS A SIXTH FORMER, AT
ST. EDWARDS SCHOOL, OXFORD.

The Bishop receives a gift from his daughter Katharine at the Cathedral, Epiphany 1955. Third from right, front row, is the Bishop's son Edward.
(By Courtesy of The Western Morning News)

THE BISHOP IN 1968

The Bishop in the Cathedral, 1970

CHAPTER I

Early Days

Robert Cecil Mortimer was born at Bishopston Vicarage, Bristol on December 6th. 1902. His father, Edward Mortimer, had been Curate of Bishopston from 1889-99 and, after spending two years in a country living, he returned to Bishopston as Vicar from 1901-11.

The family history is of much interest, especially as since 1750 the Mortimers have borne the Arms of the ancient Earls of March who had the same surname. These early Mortimers took their name from the Dead Sea (Mortuum Mare) at Mortemer-en-Brai, Normandy, where they originally had their castle. Accordingly the family Arms had tiger bars of blue and gold set around a silver sea. Some of them fought for William the Conqueror at the Battle of Hastings and by 1076 they had extensive estates in Herefordshire and Shropshire, including the town and castle of Wigmore which was their chief seat. Later Cleobury Mortimer became their Shropshire residence.

For two or three centuries the Mortimers ruled as absolute monarchs in the west and were soon married into the English Royal Family. Roger Mortimer, 4th Earl of March, was declared heir-presumptive to the throne by Richard II and, had he lived a year longer, would have been King of England! But in 1398 he was killed in Ireland and when Richard abdicated in 1399 Roger's son Edmund was only six years old. So John of Gaunt's son Henry Bolingbroke jumped the throne as Henry IV. One or two Mortimers figure prominently in Shakespeare's "Henry IV"; the troubles which led to the Wars of the Roses arose simply because Henry IV and his descendants held the throne by the vote of Parliament, whereas the nearest heirs were the Mortimers of Roger's line. The Earldom of March became extinct when Edward IV would have become by inheritance the 7th Earl.

The descent of Robert Mortimer from the ancient Earls of March has not been completely traced. But in 1750, after extensive searches and an examination of early seals and rings, still in the possession of the family, by "skilfull antiquaries", the College of Arms was satisfied that the descent of John Mortimer, Robert's direct ancestor, from the Earls of March had been established. So Robert Mortimer's Arms, as authorised by the College of Arms when he became Bishop, include, quarterly, the Arms of the Earls of March.

The Bishop's father, as shown by photographs, had a stern yet kindly countenance. An old friend of the family remembered him as "a fine vicar, very natural in manner." His wife, previously Miss Ellen Merrick, came from nearby Clifton; the couple had been married at Bishopston Church in 1890. Robert was the youngest but one of a family of three sons and three daughters; his father was 39 when he was born. The eldest son, Glanville, who was Robert's senior by ten years, was also ordained and spent a lifetime in the parish ministry. A first cousin of Robert's, Thomas Mortimer, also spent his whole life in the ministry and is now retired. Robert's youngest sister, Betty, married Prebendary R.A. Evans who was Vicar of Batheaston until his recent retirement. The Bishop's nephew, the Rev. R.M. Fookes, is Vicar of Wotton-under-Edge, Gloucestershire. The whole family were steeped in the worship and tradition of the Church of England.

St. Michael's Church, Bishopston is a grey stone edifice built in 1858, at the side of the old Gloucester Road. The Vicarage, of ornamental red brick, is next to the church. In Robert Mortimer's childhood Bishopston was already a busy suburb of Bristol. One of Robert's first memories was the sound of the electric trams - quite a new invention at the time - going along the main road outside the night nursery window. He also remembered the flickering of the little gas night-light in the bedroom.

The Mortimers at the time were modest people, yet they always had high ideals. The young Robert and his three sisters all had a rather aristocratic appearance. Their mother was a somewhat powerful person who "ran the parish", but she was very pleasant. A great influence on the Mortimer children was their wonderful old nanny, Sophia Battershill, known affectionately to the children as Baba. She and her sister originally ran a Dame School in the parish; when the sister died, Mrs. Mortimer invited her to live at the Vicarage and look after the children. A photograph shows Baba to have been grey-haired and a trifle formidable in appearance, devoted as she was to the children. She taught them to read and write, and they became much attached to her over the years. She was a very firm disciplinarian and her one never-failing weapon was "I'll put on my bonnet and leave you, Sir!"

Robert's parents loved their children, as he himself recorded: "They were very good to us, but they were very busy." There was much jealousy between Mrs. Mortimer and Baba but the children seemed to understand this and it did not greatly upset them. Baba continued to write frequently to Robert, right up to his days at Redcliffe. Her letters often began "My own dear King" - this was a nickname Robert had from early childhood. This name, one supposes, summed up the natural and relaxed elegance - one might say the episcopal air - which Robert possessed almost all his life and which perhaps reflected the greatness of those early ancestors. A number of photographs show the children healthy, full of energy, often with jolly smiles on their faces. Certainly the Mortimers seem to have had a very happy family life together.

About 1910 Robert was sent as a day-boy to St. Oswald's School, also known as XIV School, at the nearby suburb of Clifton. It still flourishes to-day as a Preparatory School; the name XIV School came from the house at 14 Apsley Road where it had been founded in 1885. After Robert had left it moved to its present larger premises at Stoke Bishop. The Bishop retained his affection for the school all his life. About 1954 he and Mrs. Mortimer visited the School for the annual Sports Day, and after presenting the prizes the Bishop delighted his audience by producing his old XIV Cricket Colours cap and wearing it for the rest of his speech!

Robert's father was a much-loved parish priest. Not only did he spend twenty years at Bishopston as Curate and Vicar, but he was very conscientious and had an exceedingly kindly nature. A friend said that Robert learned the kindness which was so much a part of him from his father's splendid example. All went well in the parish until Edward Mortimer was struck down by illness. This was obviously serious and it is significant that despite taking a lighter job he was suffering severe strokes in another six or seven years.

On his doctor's advice Edward Mortimer saw the Bishop of Bristol, Dr. G.F. Browne, and asked if he could be given a less demanding parish. The Bishop, who was very considerate, waited for a suitable parish to be vacant, and was happy to be able to offer Mr. Mortimer the Rectory of Little Somerford, a small village near Malmesbury. This meant a considerable financial sacrifice on the Mortimers' part, but the parish had a charming 14th century church with some fine oak carving and a famous screen supposed to have come from one of the side-aisles of Malmesbury Abbey. It also had a delightful Rectory in very sound condition, but most important of all the much lighter duties would give Edward Mortimer a chance to recover from his illness.

At the Farewell Presentation in Bishopston Parish Hall on November 23rd 1911, the Churchwardens presented Edward Mortimer with a gold watch, a cheque for £80 and an illuminated address in a fine morocco binding decorated in gold. Part of the address ran: "The substantial enlargement of our Parish Church, the new organ, the spacious Parish Hall, the provision for the new Church of St. Katharine's, in all costing more than £10,000 (an enormous sum for those days), are monuments of a work well done; but greater still is the love of many hearts that you have cheered, helped and led to the Source of all true Life and Strength. The ever-growing number of regular communicants, amounting to over 1,000 last Easter Day, must at this time be the source of a peculiar joy and comfort to you. You leave, Reverend Sir, a Parish well organised in its many branches, fully equipped for great future work, that will always pray Heaven to grant you a long life and a well-earned rest and peace."

A number of Edward Mortimer's former curates attended, including the Rev. C.H. Dickenson, already a Rural Dean and later to become Archdeacon of Bristol. Mrs. Mortimer was presented with a silver salver by the people of St. Katharine's Church.

So closed the first chapter in Robert Mortimer's life. His father had clearly undermined his health by the tremendously hard and devoted work he had put in, as Curate and as Vicar of Bishopston, for over twenty years. From 1902-11 he had also been Chaplain of Bristol Prison, so that the overall strain must have been very great indeed. With mixed feelings the family moved from the somewhat dreary Bristol suburb to the quiet and charming surroundings of the picturesque Wiltshire village which was now to be their home.

CHAPTER II

To Country Pastures New

Little Somerford is a delightful village, set in pleasant green rolling hills, on the northern fringe of Wiltshire. It forms the junction between three country roads. There are some rather imposing Georgian houses in the village, along with a number of those charming old cottages which so abound in the West Country. Recently some small but very tastefully designed modern houses have been added at one end which scarcely detract from the beauty of the place, adorned as it is with more than its share of leafy green trees. In 1911 the population cannot have been more than 200 or so.

The parish church, St. John's, is close to the middle of the village. It was completely rebuilt about 1300, the tower being added in the 15th century. While not exceptional in any way it has the richness of a medieval church, and within the building one senses the passing of the centuries. The nave has a fine wooden rafter roof of early date, the present timbers being of the 17th century. The splendid wood chancel screen dates from 1350, and there is a beautiful Jacobean wood pulpit. There is no memorial to Edward Mortimer in the church, but the white marble War Memorial tablet on the south wall is subscribed: "Edward Mortimer, Rector. W.R Teagle, A.F. Hiscock, Churchwardens." The church is set in a typical English village churchyard, with crumbling old gravestones amidst a pleasant grassy plot.

The Rectory was on the same road, not far from the church. A dignified grey stone house of 19th century vintage, it had large airy windows which, both upstairs and downstairs, were of the bay window pattern. Protected from the road by its long stables, it had a lovely garden including a tennis court and a croquet lawn, much in use for summer parties. The stables with their hay lofts were a delight for Robert and his younger sister Betty to play in.

Despite their regrets at leaving Bishopston the Mortimers were excited at their new country home and, until Edward Mortimer's health took a turn for the worse, had some very happy times there. Baba of course came with the Mortimers and continued to exercise her motherly care over the children. Their father became adept at croquet and loved ministering to his two hundred souls. They developed rural interests; they always had a horse or pony and Mrs. Mortimer kept a cow called Audrey. The pony and trap, in an age when cars were still at a premium, were very useful for the weekly shopping trips to Malmesbury, quiet little jaunts to nearby Dauntsey and, once a fortnight, a whole day's outing to Chippenham. The Rector became an expert gardener and was very proud of his kitchen garden - with their rather limited income, and school fees to pay, their farm and garden produce was a great help to them, especially in the War years when supplies were short. The large Rectory kitchen with its stone floor became "the dairy" and every week the children had to help to churn the milk into butter. They also kept hens and ducks and, in the style of the true old English country rectory, they almost became farmers on their modest piece of glebe.

There still survives a diary which Edward Mortimer kept for the year 1918. The entries are very brief - the Rector's health had already worsened by then - but they show him to be a man of simple country tastes, devoted to his wife and children and with a great love of Christ and his Church. A typical entry in the diary (January 12th 1918) reads: "Letter from Arthur! Good news from him. Bob has gone to the meet. Mother has gone to Sutton for Communion wine. Saw Harford cutting down the hedges round the little field. Violet coming home today." (Arthur, Robert's elder brother, had an Army Commission.) The day before he had written: "Cow getting uneasy (a later note showed that the cow had calved six days afterwards). 6 eggs today." On January 18th, evidently the beginning of the school term, he noted: "The boy has gone. Good-bye Bob!" On January 27th, a Sunday, the diary records: "H.C. 8.30 4 present. 11 a.m. M & sermon. 6 p.m. E. & sermon. One duck started to lay." A letter written by Edward Mortimer to Robert on May 18th, while the latter was working at a Harvest Camp at East Harptree, Somerset, described how Pixie, the Mortimers' pony, suddenly bolted while in the Rectory grounds, trampled over vegetables and a newly-planted apple tree and damaged her harness before Mr. Mortimer had managed to grab hold of her reins. The letter ends: "I hope you will have a happy day to-morrow. The birthday of the Church! With very much love from your loving Father."

And what of Robert himself at this time? One of his sisters described him as a very ordinary boy, often of untidy appearance with his socks wrinkled all the way down, who cycled around and played games. A favourite occupation was to cycle to the nearby station and do some engine spotting. Once he dragged his sister Betty out of a pond when she fell through the ice. This noble deed went quite unrecorded as afterwards the pair of them crept up the back stairs of the Rectory, no-one else being any the wiser! Then, as always, he was a kind and gentle person - though he couldn't bear to be teased and sometimes showed a sharp temper if fun was poked at him.

Every Good Friday the children went out with Baba to pick primroses to decorate the church - this was, of course, a custom quite prevalent at the time and Robert later continued to do this with his own children whenever he was free. In the summer he often went off on a farming holiday, partly to earn a little cash. The children used to deliver parish magazines and take 'coal money' to the poor; they were rather thrilled to do this and it gave them some insight into cottage life.

Congregations at the church were quite small; the diary reports that in 1918 there were 40 Easter Day communicants, 28 at the 8.30 a.m. Celebration and a further 12 at mid-day. The entry bears the note: "poor, but many away."

Such was life in the village, but we must remember that the children spent the greater part of the year away at school. The two elder boys went to Clifton, and by 1913 Glanville, the eldest, had commenced training for the ministry at Wells. A year later he was ordained at Swindon Parish Church. The three girls were all boarders at the Clergy Daughters' School and Robert, naturally, carried on as a boarder at XIV School. Some idea of Robert's progress there can be gained from his school reports and from the

School Magazine, though no reports before 1914 survive and the magazine did not commence publication until 1913, by which time Robert had been at the school three years. In 1913 the school comprised 65 boys in six forms, Robert then being in the 5th form.

In the Easter 1914 issue of the magazine it was reported that Mortimer ought to make a first-class hockey forward. By Christmas 1915 he was Captain of soccer and the next term he was Captain of hockey; he was also in the 1st XI at cricket. Academically he was placed 2nd in the Upper Sixth at Christmas 1915, the 1st place going to H.C.B. Mynors (later Sir Humphrey Mynors, Bt., Deputy Governor of the Bank of England) who in the same term won the top scholarship at Marlborough.

All too soon came his last term at XIV School, the summer term of 1916. Yet Robert must have looked forward to the future with happiness for in that term he won a scholarship to St. Edward's, Oxford, besides being Captain of cricket and gaining 1st place in the Upper Sixth, both on the term's work and in the school examinations. He gained a 'very good' or 'good' in every subject except Greek, at which he was 'very fair'.

St. Edward's School had been founded on very modest lines at 29 New Inn Hall Street, Oxford in 1863 by the Rev. Thomas Chamberlain. This priest had been one of the pioneers of the Catholic Revival in the Church of England. As an undergraduate he had heard Keble's famous Assize Sermon at St. Mary's in 1833 which had set the Oxford Movement into being, and he had read the well-known *Tracts for the Times.* For many years the Vicar of St. Thomas the Martyr, Oxford, Chamberlain was one of the numerous priests of those times who had to suffer considerable hardship and even persecution for their Catholic views.

So St. Edward's had always supported the Catholic wing of the Church of England, and over the years it developed from these humble beginnings to the well-known Public School which it is to-day. In the 1870's Chamberlain sold the school to the Rev. A.B. Simeon who was Warden (Headmaster) from 1870-92. It was Simeon who purchased the fine 5-acre site at Summertown, two miles north of

Oxford, where the school moved in 1873 and remains to-day. Also in 1873 the foundation stone of the School Chapel was laid. This led to an article, unfair as it was, in the *Oxford Guardian* entitled "St. Edward's School and the Ritualists." The article criticised the Bishop of Oxford for taking part in the foundation stone ceremony at which, it was alleged, the School "simply plagiarised Rome"!

The Chapel, in grey stone as opposed to the red brick of the other school buildings, is of simple design and yet lofty and impressive in its beauty. The altar was set high up - higher than it is today - and the pews faced the altar instead of facing sideways as in so many school and college chapels. The young Robert Mortimer, who was to become one of the three Chapel Sacristans, was much influenced by the fine Catholic worship of St. Edward's and for ever afterwards cherished the Catholic faith.

When Robert arrived as Entrance Scholar in September 1916 the Warden was the Rev. W.H. Ferguson, who occupied the headship from 1913-25. He was a bachelor who brought his sister with him to act as hostess and housekeeper. The sister was married to the Rev. B.W. Machin who himself did some work at the school and later commanded the O.T.C. Ferguson's reign was noted for the growth in the number of pupils. When he came there were 117 boys and on his departure twelve years later there were 235 - to-day there are over 500. When Robert arrived there were 150, all but a handful being boarders. Mortimer was assigned to Set B (the Sets being the forerunners of the Houses) under the care of W.K. Stanton. His initial form was the Shell.

Robert, always a little shy by nature, must have felt a little overawed at the move to St. Edward's. According to a contemporary, the atmosphere at the school at that time was rather "tough", in that the smaller boys were kept very firmly in their place. Possibly for this reason it was a year or so before Robert's exceptional talents began to emerge. In any case life at the school was far from normal, as it was in the midst of World War I. The teaching staff was seriously depleted, and the boys had to leave younger than normally, because of the calls of the Services. So the discipline was not as good as usual. But the situation had its redeeming features, as Bishop Mortimer himself later pointed out.

"The boys who were in the school between 1915 and 1918 were profoundly conscious of the black cloud which overshadowed them. It was a familiar experience for us to see the name of a senior prefect or prefect, who had left the school only a term or two before, appear on the panelling of the Chapel as yet another war casualty. But this experience cut both ways. It did not, in all of us, engender a sense of irresponsibility and of making hay while the sun shone. On the contrary it oppressed many of us with a deep sense of responsibility. It made us more solemn and serious than befitted our age.... On the whole the boys in the school were by no means unfortunate in the masters they had to teach them.... Indeed as I look back on my fellow prefects of 1920 and 1921, it seems to me that each and every one of us must have been intolerable prigs for our age."

Mortimer's progress at the school is covered in some detail by his school reports, by bound volumes of the *St. Edward's School Chronicle* kindly lent to us by the present Warden, Mr. Henry Christie, and by information provided by him and the School Archivist, Mr. Jack Tate. The late Col. Oliver Sturt, three years his senior as a pupil, described Robert Mortimer in his first year at the school thus: "I remember him as a pretty little boy, good and hardworking, far better at Classics than I was, but no great shakes at Maths. At this point in his life he had no athletic ability or influence in the school; later he became an excellent athlete and a powerful force for good."

Not until September 1918, when Robert moved into the Classical Sixth, is there any sign of marked achievement. In that month he was appointed one of the three Editors of the *St. Edward's School Chronicle*. He was now given scope for his very considerable journalistic talent which was to bear fruit on many occasions in later life. Had he been able to devote his whole time to it he would probably have become a highly successful journalist - but the same might be said of a dozen other talents with which the young Mortimer was so richly endowed! He continued this work for the rest of his schooldays, becoming Chief Editor in January 1920.

At this stage Robert, while making steady progress in many subjects, had not yet emerged as a brilliant scholar. As late as Easter 1920 his Classics master wrote: "He has improved in Prose Composition and Unseens, but I think him still rather weak, especially in Greek prose. His almost illegible writing is a great handicap. He can write an intelligent essay." The illegible writing came in for a great deal of stick but it improved slowly over the years.

In May 1919 Mortimer was appointed one of the three Chapel Sacristans, a coveted position which meant a great deal to him. Again he continued in this office for the rest of his school career, becoming Chief Sacristan in September 1920. A photograph of the Dedication of the Memorial Calvary (War Memorial) outside the School Chapel by the Archdeacon of Oxford on 16th December 1919 shows Robert and his fellow Sacristans robed in albs and amices beside the two officiating clergy. The future Bishop was tall and slim, handsome and dark-haired, with a very serious expression on his face. His close association with the Chapel at this time not only deepened his attachment to Catholic devotion but played no small part in crystallising his sense of vocation to the priesthood.

Another of Robert's keen interests was drama and while at school he seemed to specialise in playing women's parts! In 1918 he played Mary in "A Christmas Carol" - a photograph shows him looking amazingly like a girl, with a chubby face, clad in a long white silk dress carrying a bunch of roses. Next, in March 1919, came the role of Agnes Wickfield in "David Copperfield". "Mortimer made a very sympathetic Agnes," commented the *School Chronicle*. One of his best parts was as Viola in "Twelfth Night" in December 1919. This was the first full-scale play at the annual "Commemoration" week-end for six years. Of those who had played in the last (1913) production, all thirty had served in the Forces and two had been killed in action.

Robert's versatility extended far beyond these parts, however. On Easter Monday 1920 his performance as Lieut. David Pearson in "Diamonds" drew the comment: "He played his unpleasant part with intelligence." The

School's *History* has the amusing note, referring to July 1921: "On the fields R.C. Mortimer, having discarded women's clothing for the panoply of C.S.M. and Senior Prefect, scored 108 before lunch against Bloxham!"

In view of his later prowess in the realm of law, it is not surprising to learn that Mortimer played a leading part in the School Debating Society, of which he became Vice-President. "R.C. Mortimer spoke with his customary eloquence and persuasive style" in the School Debate, records the November 1919 *Chronicle*. Yet another sphere of office came his way in 1919 when he was appointed Custodian of the School Library.

With this wealth of academic, administrative and dramatic talent, one might have thought that Mortimer surely could not excel at sport as well. Yet we have already seen that Robert showed promise in this direction. Throughout his life, in fact, he had an intense interest in sport of almost every kind and showed marked proficiency in several games. He gained a place in the 1st XI at cricket in the summer of 1920 and, now batting at No.2, made his celebrated 108 against Bloxham in his very last term a year later. His batting performance was a little variable, but in this final term he was Secretary of the Cricket Club and scored 224 in thirteen innings, with an average of 17.23.

He also excelled at tennis and became Captain in his last year. Robert would certainly not have considered track events his speciality but he managed to win the Open Quarter Mile in May 1921.

Despite the large amount of time he gave to these activities, Mortimer's academic ability developed rapidly over his last two years at St. Edward's, though his real brilliance was not manifest, perhaps, until he reached Keble. In July 1919 he gained his School Certificate with 'credits' in eight subjects. By 1921 he had obtained, in two sittings, Higher Certificate passes in Latin, Greek, Ancient History and Literature as main subjects, with French and Scripture Knowledge (including Greek Testament) as subsidiaries.

In his last school report in July 1921 the Warden wrote: "He has laid the school and me under a lasting debt of gratitude. He and I have been very happy together - at least I have." Robert's Tutor (Housemaster) W.K. Stanton was also unstinting in his praise: "He has added one more to the list of Senior Prefects who have filled that office with distinction, and that is saying a host of other things besides. He has had a most praiseworthy career here - and none will be more sorry than I to lose him."

Robert had in fact capped his school career by gaining a Classical Exhibition at Keble in January 1921. Later he became the second old boy of the School to gain a double first at Oxford. He had been a prefect since January 1920 and Senior Prefect (School Captain) for his final term. In his last year he played a male part - Ferdinand - in "The Tempest" and spoke the welcoming Prologue before the play, always the privilege of the Head of the Sixth Form.

So ended another highly successful phase in Mortimer's career. The influence of St. Edward's on him, especially on his religious life, can hardly be underestimated. From 1920-27 "Teddies" had actually been a Woodard School, and although after that period it chose to revert to independent status, the sound Anglican teaching which had always been its mainstay continued to flourish. After a time Robert Mortimer was to 'return' to St. Edward's as a School Governor and later as Chairman. In spite of the Bishop's multitudinous preoccupations in latter years, St. Edward's remained very close to his heart.

As we have presented it here, Mortimer's years at St. Edward's seem to be a story of ever-increasing success and happiness. However, such a view would only represent one side of the picture, for right in the midst of these five years very considerable sorrow came to the Mortimers at their Little Somerford home. It reflects great credit on Robert that his school career was not adversely affected; to these events we must now turn.

CHAPTER III

College Days - From Keble to Wells

In 1916 Robert's father suffered a severe stroke. This came without any warning - if Edward Mortimer had been ill a few years previously, all the family had hoped that the quieter life at Somerford, amidst all the peace and beauty of the countryside, would have restored him to good health. But the respite was to last no more than five years.

For some months Edward Mortimer was unable to speak. Robert, kind and gentle as ever, used to sit and read to him from the "Pickwick Papers", which often gave them both considerable amusement. Bob also took over the reading of the lessons in church when he was at home, even though he had not yet developed his full height and was barely able to look over the tall oak-panelled lectern! For two years Mr. Mortimer was unable to conduct the church services and a series of locum clergy were called in to do the duties.

Anyone in close touch with the clergy will know that such a situation causes more worry to the family than it does in the case of most lay occupations. The Rector is dependent on his job for the family house. If he resigns because of illness he must vacate the Rectory within three months. Futhermore, once he has resigned it is not easy in practice to obtain another suitable parish straight away, even if his health has improved in the mean time. If, however, he decides to stay on in the benefice in the hope that his health will improve, there is always the criticism from parishioners that he is continuing to draw his salary without being able to do the work. There is the added difficulty too, of paying fees to the locums for their services, for in law, at least, the responsibility for these payments falls on the incumbent. Such worries make it difficult for the sick man to recover - it can easily seem as if the whole parish is watching him and waiting for him to pack up!

Both Edward Mortimer and his family must have felt the strain greatly. Even so the Rector fought the illness with great courage and recovered enough to take the services himself for the last year or so before his retirement. His 1918 diary shows that he was leading a fairly normal life for much of that year. He apparently took most of the services, though all the sermons on Easter Day were preached by the Rev. C.C. Simpson. He planted broad beans and artichokes, saw Bob off to school at Dauntsey, looked after the farm animals, delivered parish magazines and even grabbed the pony's reins when she bolted. In the diary he rejoiced at the Allied victories in the summer, with the hope that the hated War was going to end. Happily his son Arthur came through without serious injury.

On June 30th, however, he noted: "Had a slight attack of stroke to-night." After this the diary continued normally until July 3rd, but the pages were completely blank from July 4th-12th. Then the entries resumed fairly normally until September 11th, after which there was a complete blank until the year's end. At all events he decided that he could not continue as Rector and resigned in 1919. For a short time the family moved to a house in Nunney Road, Frome, where the eldest son Glanville was now curate of the parish church. Baba took on the job of looking after Glanville's children. The Vicar of Frome at this time was Prebendary Randolph, a fine parish priest who had a great influence on Robert and helped him to focus his thoughts about entering the priesthood.

In 1921 the Mortimers moved to 1, Princes Road, Clevedon. By this time Robert's father had a weak heart and welcomed the less hilly terrain. In 1924 they moved to a house in a still more level part of Clevedon but in 1925 they moved to Bayonne, Seaton, Devon, where Edward Mortimer's elder brother lived, as Edward was very anxious to return to the county of his birth. He had been born in 1862 at Sidmouth, ten miles from Seaton; Robert often stayed at Sidmouth for short spells in later years.

When Robert went up to Keble in October 1921 the immediate crisis over his father's ill-health was over. Family finances were somewhat restricted, however, and Robert was assisted with his College fees not only by the Classical Exhibition which he had won, but also by a grant from the Wilkes Trust. In 1726 Beloved Wilkes of Dyrham

(Beloved was his Christian name) bequeathed a farm to set up a trust to enable the son of a clergyman from Bristol Diocese to study at Oxford with a view to being ordained. Fortunately for Robert the previous beneficiary of the trust had just finished his studies at this time, and Robert was appointed in his place.

The terms of the Trust remind us that even at this early stage Robert had decided to offer himself for Holy Orders. As he put it: "I never intended or expected an academic career, I intended to be an ordinary clergyman." The vocation had developed during his time at St. Edward's, and as we have seen both the School and Prebendary Randolph were influential in guiding him to this decision. Possibly, however, the home influence may have been even greater. Robert much admired his father and kept many of his manuscript sermons, as well as newspaper cuttings relating to various stages in Edward Mortimer's career. He also had the example of his brother Glanville, who had been ordained by the Bishop of Bristol in 1914 and from 1914-16 had been curate of Swindon Parish Church before moving to Frome in the latter year. Glanville had in fact written a moving letter to Robert when the future bishop was to be confirmed at Whitsun 1917. He wrote that Confirmation would admit Robert "to the full privileges of the Catholic Church for which great Saints have lived and died . . . . As I stand before the altar to offer the Holy Sacrifice, I shall pray for you with all my heart and soul . . . . If there is any book that you would like (e.g. "The Treasury of Devotion" or "Before the Throne"), ask Mother to get it for you and I will pay for it . . . . Ever your loving brother, Glanville."

The letter shows how united the Mortimers were as a family. It shows too that Glanville, who like Robert was trained for the ministry at Wells, was of a very Catholic type of churchmanship - their father was, of course, of decidedly more moderate views.

Keble College had been founded in 1870 with the deliberate intention of preserving memories of the Tractarian Movement, and it was the only Oxford College which in 1921 still required its students to be members of the Church of England. A certain number of chapel attendances were compulsory for undergraduates, many of whom were intending ordinands. A close link had already been developed between St. Edward's School and Keble; indeed a cynical critic once described the School as "a nursery for Keble College!" On the more serious side, no other Oxford College could have provided a more suitable religious environment for the young and fast-developing Robert Mortimer.

The red-brick Keble College contrasted markedly in appearance - at any rate in those days - with the grey stone buildings, always something of a medieval ecclesiastical air, of the other colleges. Keble, which along with All Saints' Church, Margaret Street, was one of the fashionable London architect William Butterfield's major achievements, was at first sight a slightly austere structure, but the Chapel, a fine lofty building, did full justice to Butterfield's inspiration.

The Warden of Keble, who had only been appointed a year before Robert's arrival, was Dr. B.J. Kidd. His background was somewhat unusual for a College Head in that most of his previous time had been spent as incumbent or curate of Anglo-Catholic parishes. For sixteen years before going to Keble he had been Vicar of St. Paul's, Oxford. This is in no way to disparage his scholarship, for he had published a number of works on such topics as *The Doctrine of the Eucharistic Sacrifice (1898)*, *A History of the Church to A.D. 461 (1922)*, and *The Primacy of the Roman See (1936)*. Furthermore he had been Chaplain of Pembroke from 1894-96 and Lecturer in Theology at the same college from 1902-11; for most of the latter period he was also Vicar of St. Paul's. A tall, powerfully-built man, Dr. Kidd took an interest in the young Robert Mortimer almost from the day he arrived at Keble, though the Warden was so reserved by nature that for a long time Mortimer was completely unaware of this interest! When Dr. Mortimer was awarded his D.D. in 1947, Dr. Kidd gave him his D.D. robes which the Bishop continued to wear, as the occasion demanded, for the rest of his life. Kidd's Catholic outlook, which was reflected in the Chapel worship at Keble, continued the religious traditions which Robert Mortimer had first encountered at St. Edward's. He remained Warden until his retirement in 1939.

Robert was equally fortunate in his tutors at Keble. He had decided to read 'Greats' (the Honour School of Literae Humaniores or Humanities) for his degree. This School, which includes Latin and Greek prose and poetry, Ancient History, Ancient and some Modern Philosophy, is one of the most difficult, and the course normally takes four years, as against three for nearly all the other Schools. Fewer and fewer undergraduates read Greats these days, partly because Classics and Ancient Philosophy are less fashionable in the present scientific age than they were fifty years ago. In the 'twenties, however, it was held that the academic discipline of Greats formed an excellent introduction to specialised study in other fields later on. Frequently a student who knew from the outset that his real interest lay in Law or Theology would read Greats first and then a higher degree such as B.C.L. in Law or B.D. in Divinity. Mortimer's ultimate interest was to combine both Theology and Law, so the choice of Greats was most appropriate.

Mortimer's tutors included A.S. Owen, known in College as "the Crab" because of his oblique walk, who was an excellent grammarian in the Classics. Even better-known, perhaps, was W.H.V. Reade, a distinguished scholar in Medieval Philosophy. Years later, in the Exeter Diocesan Leaflet for September 1951, the Bishop added the following comment beneath a Review of Reade's *The Christian Challenge to Philosophy* which had just been published: "The author was my tutor at Oxford. He taught me what little philosophy I have learned.... I can testify to the lucidity of his mind, to his incisive irony and humour, and his profound scholarship.... He was a sincere and humble Christian. It is in gratitude and affection that I seize this opportunity of paying tribute to my old tutor and friend." These two tutors, according to the Bishop, were the weightiest on the staff and they "pretty well ran Keble between them."

Another tutor, in Ancient History, was H.M.D. Parker. He was newly-appointed and Mortimer was among his first group of pupils. "He took infinite trouble over us. I owe my 'first' to him" was Dr. Mortimer's later tribute. Parker had a house on Loch Fyne, Argyll, in most beautiful surroundings. Mortimer and other students quite often stayed there in vacations, and even after leaving college. Several letters from Parker, who signed himself "Michael", remain in the Bishop's papers, and a number of Robert's letters to other members of the family were written from The Lodge, St. Catherine's, Argyll. "We used to spend a part of the long vac. there on a reading party," the Bishop recorded, "it made a lovely holiday and I have loved Argyllshire ever since."

Another very important influence on the young Robert Mortimer was that of Dr. Kenneth Kirk, later Bishop of Oxford and a great churchman of Catholic outlook. Kirk was Robert Mortimer's moral tutor at Keble and "subsequently, bless him, he taught me all the Moral Theology I know." Later Kirk was to become one of Mortimer's predecessors as Regius Professor of Moral and Pastoral Theology and perhaps played a greater part than anyone else in shaping his career. A friendship quickly developed between the two men that continued throughout all their years at Christ Church together.

What sort of person was Robert Mortimer as he came up to Keble? His former colleagues remember him as a tall, slight, good-looking man, rather shy in manner and exceedingly intelligent. His shyness soon left him in the company of friends and he was the life and soul of many a party, yet his rather retiring manner was always part of him. A friend who was more interested in the social side of college life than in his studies remarked with envy that Mortimer was a scholar who enjoyed his work, yet he managed to play a full part in games and social activities as well!

On the sports field he took up hockey, which he had not played since leaving XIV School. At Keble he had the rather unenviable position of goalkeeper, though later he achieved distinction playing at outside left. He played for the 1st XI from 1922-25, being Captain in his last year. The College had a very strong team at the time which included several Blues. Mortimer only narrowly missed a Blue himself; he did play for the Oxford University Occasionals. In 1923 the College reached the Final of the

Inter-Collegiate "Cuppers", losing the match 0-1 to Balliol by a goal which was disputed by players and the local press as being offside. For ever after Mortimer was good-humouredly quizzed for letting in that goal, although he could not possibly have saved it!*

He also continued his cricket and tennis at Keble. He was invited to play cricket in the University Freshmen's Match in May 1922 - as will be heard later he was not very successful in this game and failed to graduate to the University side. However he contented himself with playing for the College XI. Later during his time at Keble he played for the College Tennis VI, his Captain being Lakdasa de Mel, afterwards Metropolitan of India.

Another keen interest was the College Debating Society, of which Mortimer was President in 1924. He also became a Life Member of the Oxford Union. In 1924 he was also President of Keble's Essay Club, succeeding his friend Russell Meiggs. In the same year he became the "Arch-Mummer" (President) of the Mummers, a Keble Play-Reading Society. Various dinner menus and similar items amongst the Bishop's papers include the Annual Dinners of the societies mentioned, All Souls' Junior Gaudy in 1922 and 1923 and the Commemoration Balls at Christ Church, Hertford, Worcester and New College in 1924 and 1925. They show that Mortimer was widely involved in College and University life during those years. A Keble Musical Society Eights Week Concert programme (May 31st 1922) shows the conductor to have been T.H.W. (later Sir Thomas) Armstrong, whom Mortimer was to know well later on as Organist of Christ Church Cathedral. Members of the orchestra included the then relatively little-known oboeist Mr. L. Goossens!

How about Robert Mortimer's studies amidst all this social and sporting life? His fellow-students at Keble say, almost without exception, that he worked very hard and deserved his success. Three of the Bishop's college essays which survive each bear the tutor's mark α-. A Latin translation bears the comment: "An excellent paper. Notes very good and full. In the Schools you would write in sentence form, not 'telegraphwise'." The latter remark refers to Mortimer's habit of writing very brief notes,

*A few months before his death Dr. Mortimer read the first draft of the opening chapters of this book. His only comment written on the draft was at this point, where he wrote "Oh yes he could!"

which he continued in spirit throughout his episcopate by writing many exceedingly short letters. In either case, though there might be extreme economy of words, there was no doubt as to the meaning of the acutely-reasoned and precisely-worded message.

Mortimer's first hurdle was Classics Honour Moderations, an examination coming half-way through the degree course. In this he seemed to have no difficulty in gaining a First Class. A letter of congratulation from his old tutor at St. Edward's, W.K Stanton, declared: "Evidently virtue brings its own reward - I am so delighted for you - and you must know yourself that the honest hard work which you have put in has all contributed to this excellent result."

A First in Greats was a stiffer proposition, and Mortimer had to work hard for it, although most of his friends seemed to think that he would make the grade. In his last year at Keble he shared lodgings in St. Giles with Russell Meiggs (later Classics Fellow and Dean of Balliol for many years) and Dick Walters, who afterwards became a Chartered Accountant and is now retired in Malta. The three became life-long friends and often stayed at each other's homes and spent holidays together. Mr. Meiggs comments of Mortimer at that time: "He never wavered about his career, nor about the place of the chapel in his life." Mr. Walters recalled that Mortimer, despite his brilliance, often had to struggle hard to master some of the philosophers included in the Greats course, but never gave up his determination to succeed. "I always admired him for what Aristotle would have called his $\mu\epsilon\gamma\alpha\lambda o\psi\nu\chi\iota\alpha$ (large-mindedness)," Mr. Walters adds, "never in any way priggish, he had an air of 'rightness' at all times."

In the event Mortimer got his First. A letter from Michael Parker gave the marks of the three Keble men who had taken Greats in that year (1925). Mortimer had obtained an α-, two $\alpha\beta$'s, two β++, a β+ and a β in the seven papers, which added up to a very satisfactory First. This brought a shoal of congratulatory letters, the most prized being from the Warden:

My dear Mortimer,
I am delighted to hear that you have got your First.

You would have been disappointed had the result been anything less: and so should we. But this does not lessen the distinction - nor our satisfaction and yours. You have my best congratulations. For I think you deserve your honour: and if you don't mind my saying it now, I have always been impressed by the way in which, while using to the full the opportunities which Oxford affords you, you have never swerved from your original intention of being ordained.

You will carry over with the work before you qualifications and honour that few men have: and there are great opportunities of using them before you. We want quality, more than number in the priesthood: and I am glad to think that this is your aim, and I wish you every happiness in your more immediate preparation for it, and in the work itself when it comes.

                Yours very sincerely,
                B.J. Kidd.

Another letter, from the Warden of St. Edward's, W.H. Ferguson, added: "And I just love to think that you are going to offer great gifts of mind and industry to the church. Some day you may be called upon to undertake high office - in any case to the many temptations in the life of a Priest one will be added in your case - intellectual pride: I beseech you to beware of it - or you will fail to make the best use of magnificent opportunities. This is no criticism - merely a warning which springs from a very warm affection and a keen desire that you should fulfil great promise." A friend of Robert's went even further and wrote: "Already you will feel the episcopal gaiter pressing your calf!"

Few young men can have left Oxford with more promise than did Robert Mortimer. "The bright star of the Sixth" as another former pupil of St. Edward's described him, had more than fulfilled the hope cherished for him when he went up to Keble. The years at Oxford had greatly broadened him. If still a little retiring by nature when in less congenial company, Mortimer was by now an exceedingly attractive person. A friend noted that young women were often captivated by his charm at this time. A young lady who was evidently much attracted to him wrote, on his departure from Oxford: "I shall remember you as one of the straightest and soundest men I met. Good-bye - and my wish/or yours - may your ideals remain as high as those with which you started out on the Pilgrim's Way."

Clearly Mortimer was of the stuff that Oxford dons are made of and one might have imagined that he would straightway have sought a College Fellowship. But even now he was convinced that the parish ministry was his vocation, so inevitably the next step was to spend a year at a Theological College. He chose Wells, where Glanville had trained for the ministry, and commenced his studies there in the autumn of 1925.

Wells was one of a number of small theological colleges which sprang up in Cathedral Close situations in the last century in order to give Church of England ordinands a more adequate training for the priesthood. Between the Reformation and the late nineteenth century most ordinands received very little devotional and vocational training; normally they just took a degree at Oxford or Cambridge and learned what theology and pastoralia they could in their spare time! Wells had been founded early on, in 1840, and had the advantage over some colleges in that the students lived in six or seven delightful old houses (rather than in a college block) in Vicar's Close, in the shadow of the lovely Cathedral. Robert lived at No. 27. At the end of the row was the main college building, which included a library with a lecture room above. The worship was held partly in the small chapel at the end of Vicar's Close, used by the priest-vicars in medieval times, and partly in the Cathedral. Owing to the diminishing number of ordinands the College was obliged to amalgamate with Salisbury Theological College a few years ago, and all ordination training has been transferred to Salisbury.

Among the Bishop's papers is a photograph of the staff and students taken in the summer of 1926. There were five clergymen and twenty-eight students in the picture, with Robert Mortimer, tall, handsome and somewhat self-effacing in appearance, towards the right hand in the back row. In those days such colleges had at least three staff and usually less than forty students. The small numbers and generous staff-student ratio were considered essential to give the ordinand the very personal devotional and pastoral training thought to be needed. To-day economic and other factors have resulted in fewer and larger colleges.

The Principal was Canon G.A. Hollis, an august white-haired priest who later became Bishop of Taunton. The Vice-Principal was the Rev. J.A.H. Bell and the Chaplain was the Rev. Hugh Parnell, later Vicar of Burnham-on-Sea for many years. All are now dead, and many of the students likewise, so it has been difficult to obtain many details about the Bishop's year there. However, Prebendary G.E. Tucker, who was a student at Wells during Mortimer's time, recalls that the future Bishop, with his double First, was considered one of the brightest men there: "We all knew that he would eventually reach the Episcopal bench." He describes Mortimer as intelligent, rather retiring by nature, but "he could unbend as I remember him in cricket matches and around the ping-pong table." He took part in most College activities, including cricket, hockey and tennis, at which they played sides from neighbouring towns and villages. Richard Babington, later Archdeacon of Exeter and now retired, was a student at Wells but he had left just before Robert Mortimer arrived. Quoting friends, however, he states that Mortimer, while at Wells, was by no means an ascetic! "He liked the things of this world, such as eating and drinking, but he was a man of God, a man of prayer. The influence of Wells may be seen here."

The focal point of College life was the Chapel worship, which included Mattins, Holy Communion and Evensong each day, as well as meditation and private prayer. There were also lectures, and examinations to be passed, but as Archdeacon Babington records, Mortimer found this side of the work very easy - "he soon became a formidable theologian." There would have been talks and discussions on Pastoralia; students would have conducted Sunday worship in neighbouring village churches and taken part in Missions occasionally during vacations.

With such a crowded curriculum the four terms at Wells must have passed like a flash. Some time before the year was up Mortimer had to find a vicar to offer him a 'title' or first curacy. And he could not have failed to be thrilled at the prospect, for as he wrote years later, "I was very lucky to be offered a title at St. Mary Redcliffe." This was the magnificent church in Bristol which no less a person than Queen Elizabeth I had called: "the fairest, the goodliest and the most famous church in England!"

CHAPTER IV

Ordination - and the Parish Round

The offer of the curacy at St. Mary Redcliffe came about through the good offices of Mr. Charles Clarke, secretary of the Wilkes Trust which had made a grant to Robert to enable him to go to Oxford. Not only was Mr. Clarke, who was a cousin of the then Bristol Diocesan Registrar, one of the most influential laymen in that diocese, but he happened to be a good friend of the Vicar of St. Mary's, Canon J.N. Bateman-Champain. Mr. Clarke evidently had a high opinion of Robert Mortimer, and recommended him to the Vicar in such terms that the curacy at Redcliffe was fixed up without the Bishop of Bristol ever having seen the candidate!

St. Mary's with its glorious Perpendicular architecture is a reminder of the days when Bristol was a great port and the largest and most prosperous cities in England after London were Bristol and Norwich. St. Mary's had always been the principal church in Bristol, apart from the Cathedral, and with its staff of five clergy was regarded as one of the best parishes in the city for training the newly-ordained. The church was only a short distance from the city centre and Bristol, with its 400,000 population, University, hospitals and large industrial undertakings seemed to offer every kind of experience desirable. It was also fairly close to Oxford, so that Mortimer could keep up his university contacts.

Sadly Robert's father died in 1926, just before his ordination. His death had occurred quite suddenly, within an hour or so of arriving at Weston-super-Mare, where he and his wife had travelled from Seaton by car to spend a short time at their daughter's house. The funeral, at Clevedon Parish Church, was conducted by the Archdeacon of Bristol (Ven. C.H. Dickenson, his former curate) assisted by the Vicars of Clevedon and Bishopston. A local paper commented - the resemblance to Robert will be noted - "He will be remembered as a quiet, kindly person and sportsmen who played their games at the County Ground will recall how keenly interested he was in athletics, especially cricket."

To add to the family's sorrow, Robert's mother had had to undergo an operation for cancer only a short while beforehand; they had in fact gone to Weston-super-Mare to help her recuperate. It was very unfortunate that this happened just before Robert's ordination but he decided that it would be best for him to go ahead with his plans. So on Sunday October 3rd 1926 at 11 a.m. he was ordained deacon by the Bishop of Bristol, Dr. George Nickson, in St. Mary Redcliffe. One can imagine what an impressive service it must have been, in this splendid parish church, and in presence of the great congregation whom Mortimer was soon to know so well.

The Vicar of St. Mary Redcliffe was a weighty priest who later became Provost of Newcastle and then Suffragan Bishop of Knaresborough. A Cambridge graduate, he had been Vicar of St. Mary's for fifteen years and curate of the parish for five years at an earlier stage. He had been vicar of a South African parish for three years and an Army Chaplain for the latter half of World War I. He was also a great sportsman, having played cricket for Gloucestershire and Rugby for Cheltenham College. A drawing in 1928 depicted him as tall, grey-haired and elegant in appearance, smoking a pipe with a very relaxed air. He was something of a character, with a great sense of humour; there was a large fund of anecdotes about him. He seemed the ideal vicar for Robert; the two had much in common including, of course, their love of sport.

There were three other curates at St. Mary's, being P.S. Abraham (son of the former Bishop of Derby, and himself later Bishop of Quebec); Trevor Jones who was in charge of the Mission Church and who with his wife became life-long friends of the Mortimers, and R.F. Scott-Tucker who was Precentor of St. Mary's and later Vicar of Burford, Oxon., for many years.

A photograph of the Parish Staff shows Robert with B.A. gown and hood over his cassock. He was tall, slim and handsome in appearance, with a slight air of aloofness which reflected his "very quiet and retiring manner," as a friend recalled it at the time. But even here there was another side to him. Another friend whose home was in the parish and where the new curate was a frequent visitor, describes him thus: "He was a very attractive person and we never found him shy or withdrawn. He enjoyed simple pleasures, such as family dinner and a game of rather indifferent bridge, quite as much as he did larger dinner parties and gatherings where he could match his wits and sense of fun, as well as his more serious side."

Mortimer soon became noted at St. Mary's as a preacher and almost from the start he was regarded as an 'up and coming man'. A former Churchwarden of Redcliffe, Mr. Alec Stevens, has vivid memories of his arrival:

"I recall Canon Champain.... telling the Church A.G.M. that he had offered a title to Mr. Robert Mortimer. He went on to enlarge on Mr. Mortimer's qualifications, he had obtained a double first at Oxford and had played in the Freshmen's Match when he had distinguished himself by obtaining a pair of spectacles (i.e. a "duck" in both innings!). He (Canon Champain) was much more interested in the pair of spectacles than in the double first."

Mr. Stevens was immensely impressed by a sermon Robert preached at an 11 a.m. Sung Eucharist on Easter Day:

"The church was crowded, there were masses of flowers in all the conspicuous parts of the building.... and the choir, the organ and the flowers and perhaps above all the glory of the church itself, had already suffused the whole atmosphere with the joy of Easter when Bob went up into the pulpit. He announced his text: Luke 24, v.34: "The Lord is risen indeed and hath appeared unto Simon." He went straight to his point in drawing our attention to the compassion and love manifested in this appearance to the wretched Peter, bereft of his friend as well as his Lord, weighed down by the guilt of his denial, and probably not unaffected by the suicide of Judas. If any man ever stood in need of reassurance it was the tormented Peter at that time. And in Peter's need came Christ and gave him not only the assurance of forgiveness but the joy that goes with forgiveness. Were any of us conscious of having denied

Him - and who could say other? - well Christ was here and he had the same love and compassion for us."

"That was all. I doubt if Bob occupied the pulpit more than three minutes that morning, but it was enough, it was just right. It fitted in with everything else so perfectly as though the whole of that act of worship, the liturgy, the choir, the organ, the flowers, we of the congregation, the brief and simple message we had just heard, and the church itself were all one complete design fashioned for that moment."

For a sermon to be so well remembered as that after fifty years is a remarkable tribute to the preacher! The sermon showed Robert's ability, despite his advanced academic training, to express theological truths in words that all could understand. It seems that Canon Champain must have thought his new colleague's preaching ability to be exceptional in inviting him to take his place on Easter Day, since by long tradition the Easter sermons have been the Vicar's prerogative. But a former curate of Redcliffe points out that in the 1920's the evening service was always the great preaching occasion at St. Mary's.

It seemed but a short time before the Vicar in the Parish Magazine asked the congregation's prayers for Mr. Mortimer, who was to be ordained priest by the Bishop of Bristol in St. Alban's Church, Westbury Park on October 4th 1927.

Soon after this Robert Mortimer had the sadness of losing his mother. There had been a recurrence of her malignant illness, which had now spread to her spine. Canon Bateman-Champain offered Mortimer the top flat at the Vicarage, on condition that one of his sisters gave up her job and came to nurse Mrs. Mortimer there. Previously he had been living with the other curates at St. Mary's Clergy House. Robert's younger sister Betty gave up her teaching post at Weston-super-Mare to look after her mother and the three of them moved into the Vicarage Flat. In a letter written to Robert on August 12th 1928, when he was away for a short time, Mrs. Mortimer wrote: "I am very ill. The end cannot be far off." Shortly afterwards, when they had only been in the flat for about six months, she died and Robert moved back to his old rooms in the Clergy House. His mother had shown great courage in the closing months of her life, as evidenced by witty remarks she made in one or two letters that remain.

By now the new curate was firmly estblished in the parish and deeply involved in a wide range of activities, religious and pastoral, sporting and social. His diary for 1928, in which the entries are confined to mere notes of engagements, give some idea of this. His activities included preaching at St. Mary's and elsewhere, Confessions and many interviews, Clergy School, study circles, Chapter meetings, Industrial Christian Fellowship, hospital visits, addresses at Colston's School and a girls' school, Boys' Club and Bible Class. Social events included theatre visits, whist drives, hospital and other dances; sporting fixtures including much hockey, tennis, cricket and even a little squash!

For the first few years of his ministry Mortimer wrote out all his sermons verbatim in four stiff-bound notebooks about 6"x4" in size. By this time his writing, if small, was clearly legible. The first sermon was at Redcliffe on the Sunday after Christmas 1927; even during his diaconate he preached about once a fortnight at the parish church. From the start his sermons were impressive, moving and very clearly reasoned, with an economy of words. The Easter sermon already mentioned is down in the book for Easter Day 1927, almost exactly as the churchwarden had remembered it but if anything even shorter in length! Other churches in which he preached included various ones in Bristol, Little Somerford (for Harvest Thanksgiving, 1928) and St. Paul's, Swindon, where Glanville was now Vicar.

Canon Champain, whose batting and bowling for St. Mary's Cricket Club were much missed when he left the parish, naturally encouraged sporting activities in every way, and Mortimer took full advantage of this. Hockey was the game in which Robert particularly excelled and he played in four International Trials about this time, only just missing a place in the England side. Canon Champain's successor, in congratulating him, noted that he had played for Somerset for the past two years and had scored a goal for the West against the East in the International Trial on

January 29th 1929 - he was now playing at outside left.

At a Club level Mortimer played hockey regularly for the Long Ashton side in Bristol. He was also a founder-member of the Occidentals, an 'invitation' Hockey Club for the Western Counties. Later when a Professor at Oxford he used to entertain the Occidentals when they played Oxford University or the Oxford Occasionals. For a spell in the 1950's he was President of the Occidentals. During his time at St. Mary's, he made a life-long friendship with Mr. Arthur Derrick, a member of the congregation who also played hockey for Somerset. Bishop Mortimer stayed at Mr. Derrick's Bristol home at regular intervals right up to the last year of his life; Mr. Derrick remembers him at that time as "quite outstanding.... I shall always remember the great fun we had after the games and how he enjoyed a few beers. He was a great favourite with everyone."

By March 1928 he had been appointed Captain of St. Mary's Tennis Club and in May 1929 he was able to report that the standard of play had improved considerably in the past two years. Of the Church Cricket Club he wrote: "What has amazed me during the two summers I have been playing for Redcliffe, is the few members of the parish and congregation who ever come to the ground to watch.... No gate money, your own people playing, and teas obtainable - really excellent teas, I speak from knowledge - yet practically no-one ever comes.... Try it one Saturday afternoon and it won't be the last time you'll come." (May 1929).

Mortimer's preoccupation with sport was not confined to the games he actually played. For instance he was greatly interested in the Church's three Rugby teams. The 1st XV he thought was one of the best club sides in Bristol. Of the Church School side he wrote: "The School continues to uphold its great traditions as one of the nurseries of Bristol Rugby. One boy, J. George, got his international cap and deserves our heartiest congratulations. Three boys played for Bristol. And the School won - I was going to say as usual - The Bristol Schools Championship. If anyone can find George a job, I wish they would."

Even now we have not come to the end of Robert

Mortimer's multitudinous activities in the parish, for in 1929 he undertook to revive St. Mary's Amateur Dramatic Society which had been in abeyance for two or three years. Nor have we yet mentioned one of his major contributions to St. Mary's church life as the very able Editor of the *St. Mary Redcliffe Magazine.* He took on this job when Canon Champain left to become Provost of Newcastle at the end of 1928. The Vicar was succeeded by the Rev. E.L.A. Hertslet, a bachelor who like Champain had earlier been curate of St. Mary's. After being Chaplain to Archbishop Davidson and then Vicar of Ramsgate from 1914 onwards, he was instituted to Redcliffe on All Souls' Day 1928.

In most parishes even to-day the Vicar likes to assume the Editorship of the Parish Magazine, but Edward Hertslet was very happy for Mortimer to continue. A fellow-curate remarked that although Mortimer was not gifted at small *talk*, he was very well able to *write*, not just on church or scholarly matters but also on those little human interests which lie so close to the heart of the ordinary parishioner.

As Editor, Mortimer was building on the very useful apprenticeship he had had as one of the Editors of the *St. Edward's School Chronicle.* As regards the Redcliffe Magazine he was noted for his witty and penetrating editorial notes under the headings "Footprints on the Sands of Time" and (for future events) "Coming Events Cast Their Shadows Before". We quote one or two of these to show the wide variety of topics covered.

"Sunday November 11th (is) a day which every succeeding year seems to make more impressive, to print more indelibly on the mind and heart. We observed two minutes' silence in the middle of the Eucharist, and closed it with the singing of O Valiant Hearts. So, with the sacrifice of our million dead in our minds, we pleaded before the throne of God the 'one true, pure, immortal Sacrifice', the radiance of which has fallen across their sacrifice too. At Evensong the Vicar read out the roll of Redcliffe's honoured dead." (December 1928.)

"(Whist is) a card game demanding great skill. I have to say that, because whenever I play I am badly beaten. Every Thursday night Whist Drives have been held, which members of the fair sex are allowed to attend. They have been very popular - the Whist Drives, I mean." (May 1929.)

"If the school prize-givings herald the dawn, the parish teas are the glorious sunset of Christmas. Throughout January these teas come fast and furious, treading on one another's heels . . . . It is enough to say here, that from our experience of them, the old maxim of 'enough is as good as a feast' would seem to be honoured more in the breach than in the observance. We - at least the children - prefer the feast every time, and we spell it with a capital F and conclude it with more than a capital T!" (January 1929.)

The sporting notes already quoted are from the same source, and it is not surprising that the Vicar wrote of Mr. Mortimer, when announcing his impending departure:

"(There are) many ways in which we shall miss him. Prominent among these will be his Editorship of the Magazine, and his monthly comments on current parochial affairs, which have added greatly to its interest."

The reader may think that these Magazine contributions show an exceptionally mature mind for a young unmarried priest in his first curacy. It was a mind which had an incisive grasp of human nature and deep theological issues alike. The sheer output of the future Bishop was remarkable, too, especially when one allows for the considerable time he gave to sport and social activities. He must have worked very hard, and for long hours, in this parish, just as he had at Keble earlier on. As to his devotional teaching, a generous tribute comes from the Bishop of Peterborough, the Rt. Rev. D.R. Feaver, who was formerly a parishioner of Redcliffe: "He is one of those immoveable from my remembrance and my thanksgiving. He prepared me for Confirmation, when he was a very young assistant curate, and as a boy I learnt more, and more readily, from him than anyone else."

In May 1929 Robert went on a Mediterranean cruise on the S.S. Ranchi, as the guest of Mr. Walter James. It was a very happy time, and amongst the Bishop's papers are some pencil notes of his experiences on the journey. When hundreds of miles from Britain's shores he received over the ship's radio the news that he had been appointed

Lecturer in Theology at Christ Church, Oxford. Bishop Mortimer attributed his appointment to the influence of the Warden of Keble, his former tutor H.M.D. Parker and his "Moral Tutor" at Keble, the Rev. K.E. Kirk. The letter from the Dean of Christ Church explained that the appointment would be for one year in the first instance. At the end of the year, however, the Governing Body would consider him for the permanent post of Student (i.e. teaching Fellow) of Christ Church.

In the June 1929 Magazine the Vicar of St. Mary's wrote:

"We have for some time been apprehensive that Oxford would endeavour to recall so distinguished a son into residence at the University, but selfishly hoped that the summons might be delayed a little longer. Now that it has come, however, we must join in whole-hearted congratulation to him upon the very high honour that has been paid to him. To succeed, at his age, to a post vacated by so distinguished a theologian as Archdeacon Rawlinson, is indeed a tribute to Mr. Mortimer's gifts, and to the expectations which Oxford has founded upon them . . . . He will be missed in every department of the parochial life, not least in the pulpit of Redcliffe and among the sick poor. . . .

It will be a great gain to Oxford that there should come into the rarified atmosphere of Christ Church and of the Theological Schools, one fresh from Parochial experience - the one essential training ground for understanding the application of the Gospel to human needs, and the relation of Theology to Personal Religion: where the Creed of the Incarnation of God had to be tested day by day, in its impact upon the great human problem of sin and sorrow, suffering and death."

A note added that Robert would be succeeded at Redcliffe by his cousin, the Rev. Tom Mortimer, who at the time was working for the Bush Brotherhood of St. Thomas in North Queensland, Australia.

This appointment gave some idea of Christ Church's estimate of Mortimer's academic worth, especially as he held no degree in Divinity at the time. It showed too that he had kept up his theological studies during his busy days at Redcliffe. Within a month or two - the appointment commenced on September 29th - he had left his first and only parish appointment to embark on the next stage of his career.

CHAPTER V

The Pinnacle of Christ Church

Even a scholar with so bright a record as Robert Mortimer must have felt fortunate to have been appointed to such a position. It was not just the honour of succeeding at twenty six years of age so learned a man as Archdeacon Rawlinson, a noted New Testament scholar who had gained his D.D. in 1925 and was later Bishop of Derby for over twenty years. The delightful surroundings and atmosphere - the whole environment of the place - must have seemed quite as rich a blessing as the academic standing of the appointment.

Christ Church had its origins in Cardinal College, which was founded by Cardinal Wolsey on the same site in 1525, some 250 years after the earliest Oxford colleges. The magnificent quadrangle which, with a few later additions, is known to-day as "Tom Quad" was laid out at that time. Adjoining this was the charming 12th century Monastery Church of St. Frideswide, built on the site of a nunnery founded by that saint in the 8th century. Up to the time when Cardinal College was founded St. Frideswide's Church was occupied by Augustinian Canons, but Wolsey, with the King's support, suppressed this monastery in 1525, the Church becoming the Chapel of the new college. When Wolsey fell from grace in 1529 Cardinal College was abandoned and another college founded there in 1532 had only a brief existence.

In 1546, however, Henry VIII used the buildings to found the new college of Christ Church. In 1542 the King had created a Bishopric of Oxford - it was one of six new sees where in each case the monastery church became the cathedral. So the College Chapel of Christ Church became Oxford Cathedral, or, as it is always known, Christ Church Cathedral. The Dean and Canons of 1546 took over Wolsey's buildings, staffed the Cathedral, appointed professors and set up a great educational establishment for a hundred students. The King provided a splendid Hall, one of the finest in Oxford, for the college; rather quaintly some of the roof-bosses in the Hall carry the Arms of

Wolsey's various offices including Archbishop of York, Bishop of Winchester, Prelate of the Most Noble Order of the Garter and even Papal Legate!

Owing to this unusual history Christ Church has unique constitutional features. The Head of the College, appropriately appointed by the Crown, is also Dean of the Cathedral. The Regius Professors of Divinity, Ecclesiastical History, Moral and Pastoral Theology and the Lady Margaret Professor of Divinity are ex-officio Residentiary Canons of the Cathedral, provided that they are in Anglican Orders. The College's Governing Body is made up of the Dean, the Canon-Professors and the Students.

The Cathedral, though small for such, is a delightful church, hallowed by eight centuries of worship and the site of an earlier church for 400 years before that. Evensong is sung daily as in other Cathedrals - the fact that there is less room for the congregation gives the worship an added charm and intimacy all of its own. The Shrine of St. Frideswide, a place of pilgrimage for centuries before it was despoiled in 1538, has been restored and is in the north aisle.

The Cathedral retains some interesting customs of its own. One of these is "Cathedral time", which is exactly five minutes later than Greenwich time. Thus Evensong at 6 p.m. in fact commences at 6.05 p.m. - a blessing to those who are always late! In Dr. Mortimer's time, too, the Residentiary Canons, all but one of whom were Professors, were always known as Dr. Jones rather than Canon Jones. After all whoever heard of *Canon* Pusey? - though Dr. Pusey was in fact Canon and Professor of Hebrew! Mortimer had special reason to be aware of this custom because he was the first Oxford Divinity Professor, so far as is known, who had not obtained his Doctorate of Divinity when he was appointed to the Chair. So for the first three years as Professor he was known officially as Mr. Mortimer, not Canon Mortimer, though in less formal circumstances he was quite often referred to by the latter title.

The presence of the Cathedral within the College walls has given not only Christ Church, but the City of Oxford too, an unusual distinction. Those Cambridge alumni who justifiably boast of the glorious King's College Chapel and its music have to concede that it is not a Cathedral! Indeed Christ Church is the more ancient, despite its more modest architecture, and it is the only College Chapel in England to be a Cathedral. It may be this, it may be the College's incomparable situation and lovely buildings or there may be yet some other reasons, but over the years Christ Church has come to be regarded as one of the most elegant and distinguished of all Oxford's colleges. Its past students include Gladstone and Lord Avon (Sir Anthony Eden), George Canning and Sir Robert Peel, and in the last century it was noted for its large number of gentleman commoners.

For sheer beauty and elegance of architecture the College's Tom Quad is hard to match. Its centre piece, the dignified and artistic Tom Tower, had been begun under Wolsey and was completed over a century later by Sir Christopher Wren. In the middle of the fine square lawn is the large round lily-pond, graced by a picturesque statue of Mercury added in 1928. The buildings lining the quadrangle include the Deanery and Canons' residences, the Hall and the Cathedral entrance.

Perhaps the loveliest part of Christ Church is its approach to the River Isis, which flows past the College on its south side, only two or three hundred yards from the buildings. This beautiful expanse of grass, known as Christ Church Meadows, has few equals. The more modern parts of the city are out of sight as one gazes across the level green sward to a background of the ancient grey towers of Magdalen and Merton college chapels, church spires and willow trees, scarcely changed in appearance over hundreds of years.

To all this richness of beauty, tradition and learning Robert Mortimer was sent at the early age of twenty six. Years later his great wish was to return to this college, which meant more to him than any other institution.

Only a few of the academic staff of Christ Church could surpass Mortimer for brilliance of intellect. None the less the dons included some very able theologians who did all they could to encourage the young lecturer in his studies. The Dean of Christ Church, Dr. H.J. White, was a distinguished New Testament scholar who had specialised in the Vulgate and other Latin Bible texts. He had been Professor of New Testament Exegesis at King's College, London from 1905-20, before being appointed to the Deanery in the latter year. A courtly gentleman of considerable dignity, he was somewhat Victorian in his ways. "Any change is a change for the worse" was his dictum, and he found plenty of scope for exercising it in the still conservative Oxford.

The Canons of Christ Church at this time included Dr. H.L. Goudge, Regius Professor of Divinity, who was New Testament Editor of *A New Commentary on Holy Scripture*, published under Bishop Gore's leadership in 1928. His daughter is Elizabeth Goudge the novelist. Dr. N.P. Williams, Lady Margaret Professor of Divinity, had written the essay on the Origins of the Sacraments in the well-known theological "landmark", *Essays Catholic and Critical* (1926). The Regius Professor of Moral and Pastoral Theology, Dr. R.L. Ottley, had held the Chair since 1903 and had written the essay on Christian Ethics in an earlier and even more notable landmark, *Lux Mundi* (1889). To be working alongside such scholars was a tremendous challenge to the new don.

Mortimer became a close friend of some of the non-theological dons, too. The late Sir John Masterman, who as Deputy Chief of M.I.5 in the 1939-45 War completely deceived the Germans as to where the D-Day landings were going to take place in 1944, remembered Dr. Mortimer with much regard and affection. A powerful force as a Student of Christ Church in those days, he became Provost of Worcester College, Oxford after the War. Another notable Christ Church don who knew Mortimer well was Robert Blake the historian (now Lord Blake and Provost of Queen's, Oxford). He stayed several times with the Mortimers at the Palace and gave a lecture on Bishop Phillpotts to the Exeter Clergy School. He also worked with Dr. Mortimer as a fellow Governor of St. Edward's School and was often in his company at the House of Lords. Sir Hugh Trevor-Roper, now Regius Professor of Modern History at Oxford, was a history don at Christ Church in those days; he too stayed with the

Mortimers a number of times and lectured to the Clergy School.

Mortimer very soon chose Early Canon Law as his subject for research, and was appointed University Lecturer in this subject in 1934. It seems likely that his interest in Canon Law was aroused by his friend and advisor Dr. K.E. Kirk, who at this time was Chaplain of Trinity College, and since 1927 had also been University Reader in Moral Theology - this was also to become Mortimer's special interest in a wider context.

As time was to show, this was a peculiarly fortunate choice of subject. For one thing Mortimer had a very legal type of mind - he could penetrate quickly to the heart of what seemed a complicated legal problem and, having so done, he was able to express his conclusion in words of great conciseness and clarity. Secondly, Canon Law was a topic which had hitherto attracted very few Anglican scholars, so that the path lay open for Mortimer to become a leading exponent of this seemingly abstruse branch of knowledge. Most Anglican theologians regarded Canon Law as a subject of somewhat heartless formality; many too felt that it was much more the concern of Roman Catholic scholars than any other.

On this last point, however, they would have been mistaken. For unfashionable as Canon Law had seemed in Anglican circles in the 'thirties, the whole of the ancient corpus of Canon Law was legally binding on the Church of England except those parts of it which had been set aside by Reformation and post-Reformation legislation. The only systematic attempt to formulate a body of Canon Law in England after the Reformation had been the 1603-04 Canons, which were of doubtful authority as they had never been confirmed by Parliament. Furthermore the time was fast approaching when the Church of England would completely revise her Canon Law. It was a subject of priceless value and Mortimer had chanced to take it up at the vital moment!

It hardly needs to be said that Robert Mortimer passed his year's probation with no difficulty at all and was appointed to the permanent post of Student and Tutor of Christ Church as from September 1930. In the same year he was awarded the Senior Denyer and Johnson scholarship. This was a travelling fellowship, requiring its holder to spend at least four months' residence abroad for the purposes of study. It was open to any graduate who had matriculated less than twenty years previously and was commonly competed for amongst the younger dons in Oxford. The award enabled him to travel to the Continent in pursuance of his studies, as a result of which he was soon to meet his wife-to-be.

Those who remember the Bishop in later years as apparently a rather retiring figure at parish functions would perhaps be surprised to learn that most Christ Church dons of those days regarded him as an exceedingly sociable young man! Gay, light-hearted and high-spirited, he was an attractive and handsome person, debonair and easy to get on with. He was immensely keen on bridge and continued to play hockey with great vigour for the West of England, Somerset, Oxford University Occasionals and the Occidentals. He enjoyed a glass of port amongst elegant companions, especially if they were witty conversationalists. It was noticed that he was more in the company of two colonels in the Senior Common Room, Colonel Hill who was Deputy Steward and Colonel Dawnay who commanded the O.T.C., than with the sheer academics. Indeed at this time he seemed to have a propensity for friendships with men older than himself.

So while remaining steadfast in his devotion to the Church, he enjoyed ordinary human pleasures like eating, drinking and smoking. He loved dining and wining on the High Table - a former colleague remarked humorously that Mortimer had a surprisingly ascetic-looking face for one given to such pleasures! Yet this was characteristic of the man and gave him a happy link with his fellow-humans which enabled him to overcome much of his natural shyness. At the time he had rooms in the Peckwater Quad, on the north side of the Christ Church campus.

Several former colleagues assert that Mortimer had an air of idleness about him in those days! "He must have worked very hard at Keble, perhaps he rested a bit afterwards," commented the late Sir John Masterman. "We told him that a clerical Student really ought to write something and gain a B.D. Why not do something on Gambling? This is how he came to write the book." Sir John recorded that Mortimer once said to a colleague of his, "There is one principle of conduct that ought to be observed; no gentleman works after dinner." "Are there any others?" the colleague asked. With a twinkle Mortimer replied "Yes. The second one is that no gentleman works after lunch!"

A former undergraduate of the same era added: "Very clever people often give the impression of being lazy. They have a nervous energy which gives them brilliance in flashes. The plodder works hard to achieve the same result and is jealous!" Another former Student related how (the later) Sir Roy Harrod, the economist, seeing Mortimer half-asleep on a deck chair on Christ Church cricket field on a lovely summer day, said, "I didn't know you watched cricket." "Oh yes," said Mortimer, "that's what I like about summer. There's so much to do!"

Was Mortimer's air of indolence more of a pose than anything else? He certainly liked the image, at this time, of being a debonair young man of gay abandon, as several of his former colleagues testify. Yet years later he admitted to a diocesan colleague that he was lazy by temperament, and a close relative felt that he was of rather low vitality physically for a man shouldering such heavy responsibilities. Even so there were many times in his life when his output of work might fairly have been described as prodigious. This was certainly true of the nineteen fifties and sixties when quite apart from very ably governing a far-flung diocese of over 400 parishes, he was playing a major part in rewriting the Church's Canon Law, making far greater contributions to House of Lords legislation and debates than most bishops ever manage to do, and playing a most useful part on a multitude of important committees tackling everything from prison conditions to union between Christian denominations, or from the Chairmanship of the Governors of several well-known schools to membership of the Commission dealing with the mode of appointment of bishops.

As the Student in Theology, Mortimer had the duty of acting as chaplain to the student body of the college.

Sir Hugh Trevor-Roper recalled that he was a jolly, popular, convivial chaplain - not very clerical! In this capacity Mortimer had charge of a society called "The Symposium" at which religious papers were read, often by distinguished speakers like Dr. Kirk and Mgr. Ronald Knox, and afterwards discussed by the students. An undergraduate took the chair, but Mortimer was virtually in command. "He was lucid and incisive in debate and of very firm opinion on matters like divorce," recalls a former student, "He by no means overawed undergraduates - he had no airs. In fact he took to students like a duck takes to water." A similar view was taken by a friend who wrote: "Not since the brief years of an ageing Henry Scott Holland had there been a preacher in the little Cathedral who could speak so directly and movingly to a congregation of studious young men."

There were some students who found him remote and not so easy to get on with. The reason for the apparent paradox lay in Mortimer's shyness. If his companions were warm and outgoing in manner and conversation, he excelled in gaiety, wit and charm. But faced with people who were not forthcoming and left too much of the initiative to him, his manner became reserved and there was a danger of his becoming bored. After his marriage he used to invite new students in groups to Sunday lunch at his home. A former student recalls that these were rather formal occasions, "but conversation was never difficult, though the most unlikely undergraduates were usually first asked whether they had been beagling yet!" He felt that Mortimer was not sufficiently outgoing for many to seek his advice as Chaplain, yet if they did he was very helpful. In one instance he went to great lengths to assist a student whose father had been taken ill suddenly, "raiding" every fund at the College's disposal to make sure that the young man would not be in financial difficulties. Another time, when one of his former pupils was taken prisoner in World War II, Mortimer wrote a very kind letter to the man's mother, full of Christ Church news to send to her son.

As a lecturer Mortimer was brilliant. Quite apart from the glowing accounts of his powers from many who sat at his feet, the text of many typed lectures and addresses bears unmistakeable evidence of his gifts. His style was brief, incisive and strictly to the point. His argument was always reasoned with great clarity and no words were wasted on asides. As regards sermons his speciality was the five or six minute address into which more teaching was packed than many preachers could produce in half an hour or more.

Of his college tutorials the Bishop noted modestly, shortly before his death, "I hardly had any theological pupils at Christ Church. There was A.B. (now a university professor of considerable repute) who under any competent tutor would undoubtedly have got a first, but under me only got a 2nd. My chief teaching job, and very enjoyable it was, was cramming "toughs" in elementary Latin translation." We consulted one or two of his former Honours Theology pupils, including A.B. mentioned above, and to some extent they agreed with what he said. It seems that organising the studies of Honours Theology students was scarcely his *métier*. Unlike most of the Theology tutors he supervised every branch of the subject himself, instead of delegating to other specialists those fields, such as Old and New Testament, in which he had no great expertise.

Secondly his tutorials lacked the concentrated planning needed to direct an advanced course of study in a one-hour session each week. As always he was very hospitable, and coffee would be produced if it was the right hour of the day. Quite often the first half of the tutorial would be spent in informal conversation over coffee before the student's essay ever came to be discussed. When the subject was Moral Theology or Christian Ethics he was, of course, very stimulating as a tutor, but his gifts lay in the realm of quick perception and lucid analysis and exposition, rather than in the ability to organise the studies of others.

About this time Robert Mortimer met his wife-to-be, Mary Hope Walker. Her father, Mr. J. Ronald Walker, was a barrister and the family lived in Kensington. She herself read Greats at Somerville from 1928-32, gaining her degree in the latter year. By a strange trick of fate, however, the couple first met hundreds of miles away from Oxford, amidst the gentle alpine peaks and glistening lake at the Austrian resort of Mondsee. It was August 1931 and Robert was studying manuscripts at a monastery in Salzburg to obtain material for his research project - the Origins of Private Penance - and on canon law generally. Even in those days he had a car and was driving around from place to place gaining information. Mary was spending a few weeks in Austria to revise for her degree which she was to take the following year. It so happened that they were both staying at a hillside house where an artist and his family took in paying guests during the summer. The *gasthof* was a modest one and the food was not all that might be desired. So quite often the couple walked down to the village and enjoyed a meal in a restaurant.

It was an idyllic beginning to what was to be over forty years of very happy marriage and family life for them both. One can imagine that the charm of this picturesque village, framed in the green slopes of the mountains with the moon shimmering on the surface of the lake in evening time, must have seemed little short of fairyland! The couple had much in common; both came from good Anglican families and the pattern of their education was similar. Mary had been a pupil at Wycombe Abbey School before going to Oxford, and having read Greats she shared with Robert a 'professional' interest in the Classics and Humanities. Both had a gentle, kindly nature and they were keenly interested in cultural pursuits. Their gift of hospitality and generosity towards friends ensured a happy life ahead of them.

The one sad event during their courtship was the untimely death of Mary's father in 1932, a year before their marriage. But at least Mr. Walker had the chance to get to know his future son-in-law, and he complimented Mary on her choice by saying that Robert was quite the nicest young man she had ever brought home! The couple were married at St. Mary Abbots Church on July 13th 1933 by Bishop E.J. Palmer, a friend of Robert's who had formerly been Bishop of Bombay. Robert was 30 years of age and his bride 23.

Thus were united two families of great academic distinction. Mary's mother was first cousin to

Dr. F.W. Pember, who was Warden of All Souls' from 1914-32 and Vice-Chancellor of Oxford University from 1926-29. The two sons and two daughters of the marriage are all graduates, and two of them gained Firsts at Oxford. Mark, the eldest, is a master at Shrewsbury, Sophia is married to a university lecturer in the U.S.A., Edward (who gained a Fellowship of All Souls') is a leader writer for *The Times* and Katharine is a member of the Central Policy Review Staff (formerly Lord Rothschild's 'Think Tank') in Whitehall - her husband is a university lecturer. Despite the stern demands on Dr. Mortimer's time they were blessed with years of happy family life.

CHAPTER VI

The Later Years at Oxford

Although Robert Mortimer at this stage had only completed four out of nearly twenty years at Christ Church, it is a convenient point to divide the chapters. For the first six years of their married life the Mortimers lived at 91, St. Aldates, in the busy main street. It was a small house opposite the Meadow Gate, originally intended for the Dean's coachman! In a city where accommodation was increasingly short, however, many young married dons lived in houses of this kind. A good deal of entertaining is always involved in the life of an Oxford teaching fellow, and here Mrs. Mortimer excelled. University staff, tutorial pupils, new students and many other categories of people had to be entertained, especially in a college like Christ Church. This was a good apprenticeship for later days at the Bishop's Palace.

In 1933 Robert Mortimer's first book, entitled *Gambling* was published. It was one of the 'Standpoints' series edited by Dr. Kirk and published by the Centenary Press. A rather brief work of 124 small pages, it was not reviewed in the more serious theological journals. At the same time it was lucidly written and carefully argued, like all his works. Mortimer took the view, similar to the Roman Catholic position, that gambling has an amusement value which is perfectly legitimate for Christians as long as it is not actuated by covetousness or carried to excess - there is *no theological objection* to gambling as such. He maintained this view all his life, despite the fact than many Christians of Protestant shades of churchmanship were strongly opposed to any form of gambling, even a penny raffle at a Church bazaar.

Bishop Mortimer's sense of fun often came out, in fact, when this topic was being discussed. Sometimes when a speaker expressed his horror at the 'evils' of gambling, the Bishop would say, with a twinkle in his eye: "Well, as a matter of fact I myself make a regular income out of gambling!" He would then explain that he was referring to the royalties he made on the sale of this book! At the

Diocesan Conference, just after the issue of Premium Bonds had been announced, the then Bishop of Plymouth, an Evangelical, expressed from the platform his strong disapproval of the idea. Whereupon Dr. Mortimer, in kindly tones with the suspicion of a smile said: "Despite what the Bishop of Plymouth says, I think it is a good idea and I am going to buy some." He had previously enjoyed a joke with Archdeacon Thompson, who said of church folk, "they strain at a raffle and swallow an insurance policy!"

Despite the advice of his colleagues mentioned above, Mortimer did not submit the book for the B.D. degree - it was too short a work. He did however gain the B.D. in 1938 with a Dissertation entitled *The Origins of Private Penance in the Western Church*, which was published as a book in 1939 by Oxford University Press. This was a scholarly work of 190 pages which was well reviewed in the theological journals. He refuted the view of Galtier and others than a system of private penance existed alongside the rite for public penance in early times, his thesis being that private penance (Confession) arose through modification of the earlier system of public penance. He argued his case with great clarity and precision. Although his treatment was inevitably legalistic, he showed much common sense and humour in the book, which remains an authority on this rather specialised subject.

Mortimer had already been University Lecturer in Early Canon Law for five years by now, and this book considerably enhanced his academic reputation. In the same year, 1939, he was chosen by the two Archbishops as one of the fourteen members of the Archbishops' Commission on Canon Law, of which Dr. Garbett, then Bishop of Winchester, was Chairman. The Commission included several Bishops and Deans, Mr. Justice Vaisey, the Chancellor of London Diocese, and the Regius Professor of Ecclesiastical History at Christ Church, Dr. Claude Jenkins. Even so, Mortimer's knowledge of Canon Law could measure up to that of any of the clergy on the Commission. The purpose of the Commission was to prepare the way for the complete rewriting of the Church of England's Canon Law.

During the years 1934-39 there had been several

changes in the home and college situation. In 1934 the Mortimers' first child, Mark, had been born, followed by Sophia two years later. The proud father was unable to attend Mark's Baptism in Burford Parish Church because the Dean of Christ Church, Dr. White, had died a few days before and his funeral was at the same time as the Baptism. But Mortimer did have the privilege of baptising Sophia at the Cathedral.

The new Dean was Dr. A.T.P. Williams who after gaining a Fellowship of All Souls' had spent the whole of the period 1915-34 on the staff of Winchester College, latterly as Headmaster. An able theologian, he was best known, perhaps, for his work as Chairman (from 1950-68) of the Joint Committee which produced the New English Bible. Within five years of his appointment to the Deanery he had become Bishop of Durham.

Mortimer was greatly influenced at this time by Dr. Kirk. Kirk had a brilliant intellect and his monumental work *The Vision of God* (his Bampton Lectures, published in 1931) must rank as one of the greatest Anglican contributions to Moral Theology of all time. As early as 1920 he had published *Some Principles of Moral Theology* which, apart from Skinner's *Synopsis of Moral and Ascetical Theology* (1882), was the first substantial work on Moral Theology by a Church of England author since the great blossoming of the subject in the 17th century.

Kirk virtually revived the study of Moral Theology, as far as the Church of England was concerned. It was largely through his influence that the Regius Chair of Pastoral Theology, founded in the 19th century to give pastoral training to Oxford ordinands at a time when few of them went to Theological College, was restyled the Regius Chair of Moral and Pastoral Theology. The coming of the Theological Colleges had rendered the original purpose of the Chair obsolete, and Kirk's researches had given a new importance to Anglican Moral Theology. Kirk succeeded to this Chair himself when Dr. Ottley vacated it in 1933.

It was natural that the friendship between the two men who had so much in common should deepen over the years. Both were of impressive height and physical stature and both had exceptional gifts of perceptiveness and clarity of expression. If Mortimer was a little shy in manner, Kirk was more so, and admitted very few of his friends to any great personal intimacy. Kirk had much admiration for his younger colleague and was almost a second father to him. On Mortimer's own showing it was Kirk who first interested him in Moral Theology and in a very real sense he became Kirk's successor in this important field of knowledge. He did not immediately succeed Kirk in the Chair of Moral and Pastoral Theology, for on Dr. Kirk's appointment to the See of Oxford in 1937 Dr. Leonard Hodgson held the Chair from 1938-44. But co-operation between the two theologians was always close and became more so in 1934 when Mrs. Kirk tragically died of pneumonia in early middle age. While Dr. Kirk was caring for his wife and five children during this illness, Mortimer acted as his deputy and undertook many of his teaching duties. When Kirk became Bishop of Oxford he often sought Mortimer's advice, and one of the latter's theology pupils at the time remarked that tutorials were often interrupted by telephone calls from Dr. Kirk!

By now the shadow of the Second World War lay on the horizon. The work of the University went on, as far as possible, during the War, but the conflict inevitably brought sweeping changes to college life. Only undergraduates reading science or medicine, apart from those medically unfit, were exempt from call-up. Student numbers did not fall too greatly, since many young men reading non-scientific subjects were able to put in a year's residence at college before being called up. Christ Church was in fact overcrowded during the War years, since many undergraduates from Brasenose were resident there, Brasenose having been taken over by a Government department. A good many Christ Church dons were young enough to be called up and substitutes had to be found. Male staff of almost every description became increasingly difficult to obtain.

However, Dr. Mortimer, like all the clergy, was exempt from military service and so found himself taking on some unexpected jobs for which, as he put it with altogether undue modesty, he was quite unqualified. At the start of the War it was thought best for Mrs. Mortimer and the children to move to her mother's house at Burford, though by a strange irony the only bombs which fell in the area were near Burford - they came from a single German aircraft and no-one was hurt.

So they left 91 St. Aldates and Mortimer took rooms in the college. From 1940-44 he was Junior Censor of the House (as Christ Church is always known to its members) and occupied the Junior Censor's rooms in Tom Quad. The Senior Censor was Alex Russell; the Censors were the disciplinary officers, corresponding to the Deans of other Oxford colleges.

More formidable, probably, were the duties of Acting Steward which Mortimer twice took over for short periods. The first occasion was on the death of the Steward, Sir John Percival, in 1944. In 1946, when Professor, he again took on these duties after the Acting Steward became ill and later died. The Steward was Domestic Bursar; his duties included keeping the household accounts of the college, responsibility for sending accounts to students and staff for meals and drinks consumed, and in general seeing that the House, as regards these aspects, lived within its means. Unlike many scholars Dr. Mortimer had an able grasp of accounting principles which was to bear fruit many times during his episcopate. V.F.A. Mason in the 1977 issue of *Christ Church* wrote: "These two (Russell and Mortimer as Censors) with the Dean, Treasurer and Steward ran the House for five years of overcrowding and rationing, which tried Mortimer more than the others." Sir John Masterman told the present writer, in fact, that during those years Mortimer "virtually ran Christ Church." When later appointed Professor he continued to serve as Air Raid Precautions Officer and for a time he looked after the parish of Alvescot while the incumbent was away.

These extra responsibilities made Mortimer more than ever attached to Christ Church. They demonstrate too the very great output of work, demanding widely different skills, of which he was capable, despite any impression he may sometimes have given to the contrary. Nor did his studies lapse during this time. Mortimer's reputation as a Canonist grew steadily over the War years and even in the early 'forties the Archbishop of Canterbury was seeking his advice. He had been appointed a member of the Archbishops' Commission on Kindred and Affinity and in January 1940, after the Commission had reported, Archbishop Lang wrote to him: "(The report) is a work of real and permanent value. Your great knowledge of the Canonists was of special value to the Commission and your Appendix forms a most important addition to the volume. Please accept my most real personal thanks."

In March 1943 Mortimer received a query from Lang's successor William Temple, through his Domestic Chaplain the Rev. Ian White-Thomson. The letter asked what was the position in canon law of Marriage by Proxy: "Will you tell his Grace what were the leading principles governing it in the Church? The whole question is becoming rather live at the moment, and people are beginning to ask what the C of E says about it." Attached to the letter was a copy of Mortimer's answer - an eight-page typescript setting out an intricate but carefully-reasoned legal argument, with many historical references.

In 1943 Mortimer was elected as Proctor (representing Oxford University) in the Convocation of Canterbury, an office which he retained until his appointment as Bishop of Exeter in 1949. Although as a member of the Commission he had already played an important part in the Church's deliberations on Canon Law, his voice had only been heard so far in the privacy of the committee room. From now onwards he had the chance to speak, especially on matters concerning morals and canon law, on the Church's principal legislative bodies.

In 1944 Professor O.C. Quick, who held the Regius Chair of Divinity at Oxford, died and the Chair was offered to, and accepted by, Dr. Leonard Hodgson who at the time was Regius Professor of Moral and Pastoral Theology. So the Crown had the task of finding a suitable candidate for the latter Chair. It is hardly an exaggeration to say that the choice of Robert Mortimer was almost inevitable. Not only was he already highly respected on the Oxford scene, but his knowledge of Canon Law was unrivalled amongst Anglican divines. It was unusual, certainly, that he had not yet gained his Doctorate of Divinity - in fact some Chairs of this kind were once limited by statute to those holding the D.D. degree. The sole reason for this state of affairs was that higher doctorates are normally awarded for published works, and Mortimer had not yet written a second scholarly work which would have qualified him for the degree.

It was scarcely a surprise therfore, when on January 28th 1944, Mortimer received a letter from the Prime Minister's secretary offering him the Professorship. He accepted and on February 4th a letter arrived, signed personally by Winston Churchill, announcing that the King had approved his appointment to the Chair and the Canonry of Christ Church.

The Mortimers now moved into the attractive Canon's House on the edge of Tom Quad, and the new Professor gave up the post of Junior Censor. As Residentiary Canon he had the usual share of Cathedral duties and was often to be seen reading a Lesson at Evensong on weekdays at 6 p.m. The family were glad to be living all together once more. There were now three children, a second son, Edward, being born to Mrs. Mortimer late in 1943. Katharine was born in 1946. The two boys were educated at Summer Fields, Oxford and at Eton, both boys gaining second place for their year in the Eton Scholarship examination - surely a family record? Sophia was at Cotter's Bow, Burford before completing her schooling at the Beehive School, Bexhill-on-Sea, whilst Katharine was educated at the School of St. Mary and St. Anne, Abbots Bromley.

By way of welcoming them to the Cathedral Chapter the Dean and the other Canons invited the Mortimers to tea at their various houses in Tom Quad. The Dean at the time was Dr. John Lowe, a Canadian, who was at the Deanery from 1939-59. He had taken a First in Greats at Christ Church in 1924 and a First in Theology in 1925. Returning to Canada he became Professor of New Testament Language and Literature at Trinity College, Toronto (his original university) in 1929, where he remained until his appointment as Dean. A big-built person, grey-haired yet looking younger than his age, he had a kindly manner and his Canadian accent at Cathedral services was a refreshing change. The other Canons included Dr. Hodgson and Dr. Claude Jenkins, the eccentric bachelor so colourfully described by Elizabeth Goudge in her life-story.

As a Canon-Professor, Mortimer was now a senior member of the Governing Body of Christ Church and, showing that wisdom on committees which was so characteristic of him, did much to heal the old rivalry between the Canons and the Students. Until the 19th century the Canons alone had governed the College, the Students having no say at all. So a delicate relationship existed between the two groups and there were certain matters which inevitably tended to divide them. For instance the Cathedral cost the College thousands of pounds a year to run and some of the Students, particularly those with no Church affiliations, might question whether such expenditure was really necessary. Problems could also arise over the staffing of the Cathedral. In earlier times all the Residentiary Canons had been Theology Professors, whereas in recent years the Diocese of Oxford has naturally pressed for Canons having purely diocesan duties. In Mortimer's time at Christ Church the Archdeacon of Oxford held the only such canonry, but to-day there are two diocesan Canons as well as the four Canon-Professors. In all such matters Mortimer's tact and understanding did much to promote a sense of unity amongst members of the Governing Body.

In 1946 Canon Mortimer was appointed Examining Chaplain to the Bishops of Salisbury and Bristol, which showed his increasing influence. He had been Examining Chaplain to the Bishop of Ripon since 1931; Dr. Burroughs, the Bishop, had been Dean of Bristol from 1922-26 and had known Mortimer well for many years.

1947 was to be an important year, for it was then that Mortimer published his best-known work, *The Elements of Moral Theology*. This was a notable contribution to scholarship and within months he was awarded his Doctor of Divinity degree. The title of the book was similar to that of Dr. Kirk's *Some Principles of Moral Theology* but Mortimer's approach was quite different, being in many ways a natural sequel to what Kirk had written. Kirk had adopted an empirical and logical approach and his field was very wide, including such topics as Faith, the Christian character and the education of the soul, besides Christian Ethics and Penitential Theology. Although Dr. Kirk quoted much from the Scriptures, Aquinas and the 17th century Anglican divines, he tried to avoid dogmatic and authoritarian statements as far as possible. Kirk described his book only as a "tentative work" and said that an immense amount of work remained to be done.

Mortimer, strangely enough, used almost the same words about his own book when in the Preface he called it a "tentative sketch or framework" for an Anglican Manual of Moral Theology which he hoped someone would write later on. He again remarked that " a great deal of work needs to be done before this is possible." He dedicated his work to Kirk, "to whose book, teaching and friendship I owe more than I am able to express."

Mortimer went much further than Kirk towards producing a systematic, authoritative treatment of morals on the lines of the Roman Catholic manuals. In fact it is surprising how much he managed to codify in a relatively small volume. He made far more use of Aquinas than of the Scriptures or any other work, though Aquinas himself, of course, made very great use of the Scriptures. Mortimer also quoted Anglican moralists Richard Hooker and Jeremy Taylor and the Roman manuals of Prümmer and Merkelbach, but on the whole he gave little weight to Roman Catholic scholars after Aquinas.

Though much of his treatment was inevitably legalistic Mortimer adopted a very positive approach by giving much space to the seven great virtues Faith, Hope, Love, Fortitude, Temperance, Justice and Prudence. Reviews of the book varied from those who claimed that it was far too technical to be understood by most Christians, or too akin to Roman Catholicism in its approach, to those who acclaimed it with enthusiasm as the greatest step forward in Anglican Moral Theology for very many years. In fact the much hoped-for Anglican Manual is unlikely to appear in our lifetime because in recent years the trend of Christian thought has moved away from authority and legalism in morals to the so-called Situation Ethics, where the Christian in a spirit of prayer and love decides for himself what is the right course of action to take. But in Canon Demant's words (1948) Mortimer's work was "the first corpus of teaching of its kind from the pen of a recent Anglican theologian." By any standards it was a landmark in the progress of Anglican Moral Theology.

In the very same year Mortimer produced an extensively revised edition of another learned book, Canon T.A. Lacey's *Marriage in Church and State*. He had known Canon Lacey quite well in earlier years, since his son had been co-editor with Mortimer of the *St. Edward's School Chronicle*. Canon Lacey, long since deceased, had published the work - an expert treatise on the Christian Doctrine of Marriage and on the Marriage Laws in different countries - in 1912 originally, and the book had long been out of print.

Mortimer's revision was unusual in that on several matters he had expressed opinions which he knew differed completely from Canon Lacey's own views. In the Preface to the 1947 edition he made it quite clear in what parts of the book he had done this, adding that "Canon Lacey's inimitable style and vigour will make it easy for even the most inexperienced of higher critics to distinguish "L" from "M", and it is not likely that Canon Lacey's reputation will suffer from the attribution to him of any error of mine!" In fact Mortimer had rewritten something like half the book.

This book remains a standard work on the subject of Marriage; it was reprinted in 1959, although Bishop Mortimer did not find time to revise it again to cover the big changes in English Divorce Law in 1969. Indeed if Dr. Mortimer had not become a Bishop, his output of written works might have been very considerable. On his appointment as Bishop of Exeter, however, not only was a great part of his time taken up with diocesan and central Church commitments but he felt it his duty, as a Bishop with expert knowledge of Christian Morals, to give much time to Parliamentary and Committee work. In this way his great learning benefited Church and nation through personal contact and advice rather than through books.

Also in 1947 the Report of the Canon Law

Commission, referred to on page 49 was published. Its excellent short history of Canon Law from earliest times broke completely new ground as regards the Church of England, and Mortimer had contributed as much towards this as any member of the Commission. Also included were 134 proposed new Canons and a Memorandum on the meaning of "lawful authority" by Mr. Justice Vaisey. Although 25 years were to pass before the proposed new Canons, after much modification, received the Royal Assent as a revised code of Canon Law, it was recognised at once that a solid new foundation had been laid after centuries of stagnation.

So Mortimer's stature in Church and University circles continued to grow. Every year now he was offered more public offices. He was delighted to be appointed a Governor of St. Edward's School in 1947, a position he held until his death in 1973. Also in 1947 he was chosen as Select Preacher to Cambridge University. In 1948 he was appointed Provost of the Midland Division of the Woodard Schools and Provost of Denstone College.

The present writer had the privilege of attending several meetings of the Oxford University Church Union (the University Anglican Society), of which Dr. Mortimer was President, in his rooms in Tom Quad about this time. The meetings usually began with a talk by a visiting speaker such as Bishop Kirk or Professor Hodgson, which was followed by discussion. The room in which meetings were held was elegantly furnished, and often coffee was hospitably provided. By now Dr. Mortimer was very impressive in appearance. Tall and handsome, with slightly greying hair, he had something of a patriarchal air about him as he presided at these meetings. He did not talk a great deal himself but encouraged students to speak their minds. At the appointed hour the discussion would be brought firmly to a close and the company would go to the Cathedral for a short service of prayer. Meetings were also held at other colleges.

During his later years at Oxford Dr. Mortimer maintained a close link with ordinands by lecturing on Moral Theology at St. Stephen's House, the Anglican Theological College. A former student there recalls that, in contrast to his often brilliant public lectures, Mortimer appeared to speak with some diffidence in this smaller, more intimate, circle. He was sometimes difficult to hear and would occasionally say: "You can take this down if you wish - it's up to you."

In 1948 the Bishop of Blackburn, Dr. Askwith, took the very unusual step of appointing Mortimer Chancellor of the Diocese. There had been clerical Chancellors in earlier days; Canon 127 (1603) did not require the Chancellor to be a barrister or solicitor but "of the full age of 26 years at least, and one that is learned in the Civil and Ecclesiastical Laws, and is at least a Master of Arts, or Bachelor of Law, and is reasonably well practised in the course thereof." Mortimer fitted these requirements comfortably. In modern times, however, owing to the increasing complexity of the administration of the law, Chancellors have almost always been professional lawyers - usually barristers of some seniority and often Queen's Counsel. After all the Chancellor has to sit as judge in the Consistory Court and is constantly making legal decisions, e.g. in the granting of Faculties, for which the expertise of a barrister or solicitor would seem well-nigh indispensable. The new Canon G2 (2) in fact specifies that the Chancellor shall be "at least 30 years old and either a barrister at law of at least 7 years' standing or a person who has held high judicial office."

Mortimer, learned as he was in Canon Law, was neither barrister nor solicitor, nor had he previously held judicial office. How successful was he as Chancellor? Owing to his early appointment as Bishop Dr. Mortimer only held the office as Chancellor from September 1948 until April 1949, but the Registrar of Blackburn Diocese, Mr. Leslie Ranson, has kindly consulted correspondence relating to this period and reports as follows:

"It is clear that a very happy relationship was developing between them (Dr. Mortimer and Mr. Clayton, the then Registrar of Blackburn Diocese).... When discussions were taking place between my predecessor and Bishop Askwith about the appointment of a successor, the Bishop expressed doubts as to the wisdom of appointing another clergyman and Mr. Clayton replied in the following terms: 'I do not share your anxiety about appointing another Cleric. I am sure the legal profession would not worry. The present short time has been so full of good meat and I feel a real sense of loss, there has been such a kindly (even humorous) touch. . . . . Personally I feel Blackburn should have a sound Churchman and I would far rather he be Cleric than Lay if the Laity cannot muster the right article.'"

In the event the laity did muster the right article. Mr. R.A. Forrester, a barrister, was appointed and was a splendid Chancellor from then until his death in 1976. None the less this is a remarkable tribute to Mortimer's legal ability, tact and understanding. It squares with a comment made by Sir John Guillum Scott, former Secretary of the Church Assembly: "He (Mortimer) was a brilliant Advocate and a most cogent and persuasive speaker; clearly he would have done well at the Bar." While one or two clergy who were also barristers, such as the Rev. E. Garth Moore and the Rev. K.J. Elphinstone, have held Diocesan Chancellorships since then, it seems probable that Mortimer may have been the last purely clerical Chancellor in the Church of England.

By this time it was a virtual certainty that Mortimer would become a Bishop. The Church of England was about to revise her Canon Law and it was vital to have an expert on this subject in the House of Bishops. Mortimer's knowledge of the Canons was without equal amongst Church of England clergy and quite apart from this his fine appearance and gracious manner, his brilliance of mind and unaffected elegance, not to mention his devotion to the Church, made him an ideal candidate for the Episcopal Bench. The only question was - when? At his first Diocesan Conference at Exeter Dr. Mortimer said that he had expected to be appointed a Bishop in another five years. However 1948 was only just out when he received the following letter:

Confidential

        10 Downing Street,
        Whitehall,
        24th January, 1949

Dear Sir,
  The See of Exeter is vacant by the

resignation of Dr. Curzon, and it is my duty to submit to The King the name of a successor.

After the most careful consideration, I have come to the conclusion that I cannot better serve the interests of the Church than by offering you the succession to this See. On hearing from you that you would be willing to accept, I shall be happy to submit your name to The King.

Until His Majesty's approval has been obtained, I trust that you will treat this proposal as confidential.

            Yours sincerely,
            C.R. Attlee

The Reverend Canon R.C. Mortimer, D.D.

CHAPTER VII

Consecration and Enthronement

From that moment matters went ahead rapidly. Dr. Mortimer indicated his willingness to accept the See and on February 10th news that the King had approved the appointment appeared in the press. On March 3rd he was unanimously elected to the Bishopric by the Dean and Chapter of Exeter Cathedral. On April 22nd Dr. Mortimer's election received formal confirmation in London and on St. Mark's Day, April 25th 1949, he was consecrated Bishop in Westminster Abbey.

The Consecration of a Bishop follows the same pattern as a Priest's Ordination, but it is more solemn and majestic, nearer to the Coronation Service in its atmosphere. Of the various churches in Canterbury Province where Bishops are consecrated, which include Canterbury, St. Paul's and Southwark Cathedrals, surely none could provide a more splendid setting than Westminster Abbey, the church in which Kings are crowned. And as it happened the Archbishop of Canterbury, Dr. Fisher, who consecrated Dr. Mortimer to the Episcopate, was to crown the Queen in the same church only four years later, Dr. Mortimer then being in the congregation.

The preacher at the service was another of Dr. Mortimer's Oxford friends, Dr. Austin Farrer, who had succeeded Dr. Kirk as Chaplain of Trinity College and was later to become Warden of Keble. A quiet, ethereal and scholarly divine, he preached an eloquent sermon, on classic Catholic principles. "A bishop is given to his people, he is no more his own. His business is to make men Christians and to keep them Christians. That is the beginning and end of his task, and against this standard must he be constantly measuring the multifarious workings of his diocese, and the use which he makes of his own time."

At the moment of Consecration the Bishop-elect knelt before Dr. Fisher, who was vested in a gold cope and mitre sitting in his chair, while the Bishops Assistant, fifteen in number, formed a great circle of scarlet as they moved up and, with Dr. Fisher, laid their hands on the head of the new Bishop in the manner that goes back over seventeen hundred years. Dr. Mortimer had been presented to the Archbishop by the Bishop of Oxford, Dr. Kirk, and the Bishop of Derby, Dr. Rawlinson, who had been Mortimer's predecessor as Student of Christ Church.

At the Communion which followed the new Bishop, after the Archbishop himself, was the first to receive the sacred elements. The Bishops then received Holy Communion, followed by Mrs. Mortimer and the near relatives. At the end of the great service the processions filed out and the great bells of the Abbey rang out their joyous welcome to the new Bishop of Exeter.

A month was to pass before Dr. Mortimer was to be enthroned in Exeter Cathedral. Three days before this, on May 24th, he was received at Buckingham Palace to do homage to the King. On May 26th, the Bishop and Mrs. Mortimer motored down from Oxford and stayed the night at Bishop's Court, Sowton, five miles from Exeter. It was an ancient custom that new Bishops of Exeter spent the night before their Enthronement at Bishop's Court, an old manor house built in the first place by Bishop Bronescombe, who was Bishop of Exeter from 1258-80.

The next day, Friday May 27th was the day of the Enthronement. And what a glorious building was the Cathedral Church of St. Peter! Although rather small compared with most Cathedrals, Exeter Cathedral gives the impression of great length. Its inspired architects placed the Choir Screen far forward, so that as one peeps through the gaps in the screen one sees no less than seven great bays beyond the entrance to the Choir. And the sheer geometric beauty of the unbroken line of Gothic vaulting of the roof of the Nave and Choir (at 300 feet the longest in existence) is scarcely matched anywhere else on earth! The richness of the lovely Decorated architecture of the Nave itself has but few equals, and outside the two large Romanesque towers, the only part of the old Norman Cathedral to be left standing, give great weight and dignity to the building.

The first part of the ceremony was at Eastgate, where

a procession of civic dignitaries arrived from the Guildhall for the Mayor to present the new Bishop with an illuminated address of welcome. By a happy coincidence - or was it intended? - the Mayor, who had only been formally elected the day before (Major-General W.G. Michelmore), was the Diocesan Registrar. So he had a special interest in the new Bishop and was to work very closely with him for twenty years, not only in the Diocese but on central Church committees.

From Eastgate the procession moved to Broadgate, where the Bishop of Crediton, the Rt. Rev. W.F. Surtees, presented Dr. Mortimer with his pastoral staff or crozier, the symbol of his authority as Chief Shepherd of the Diocese. Scholars from Exeter Episcopal Boys' and Girls' Schools presented an address of welcome. The procession then made for the Cathedral for the Enthronement Service which followed the traditional pattern. The Bishop rapped three times on the door with his crozier to gain admittance, and was greeted by a fanfare of trumpets as he entered the building. The Dean, Dr. S.C. Carpenter, welcomed him and the Bishop asked to be "canonically inducted, installed and enthroned." Prayers were said for the new Bishop, splendid hymns were sung. The actual Enthronement, as always in the Southern Province, was performed by the Archdeacon of Canterbury, in this case the Ven. Alexander Sargent, acting as the Archbishop's representative.

The Bishop's Throne, surely the finest in the land, had not been brought back from Mamhead, where it had been stored during the War years to protect it from bomb damage. So a temporary throne had been constructed which included the base only of the real one. The latter was fully restored to the Cathedral three months later.

Dr. Mortimer preached two sermons during the service. The first, given from the Choir pulpit, was on 1 Timothy 6, v. 20: "Keep that which is committed to thee." To worship God and to keep his Commandments was the first and whole duty of man and it was the heart and soul of all that our fathers had to hand down to us. The second address, from the Nave pulpit, was on the Feeding of the Five Thousand, with the text "Give ye them to eat"

(St. Mark 6, v.37) "What the Lord said to the disciples," the Bishop began, "he has said to each of us clergy. We are to feed the flock of Christ . . . . It is our high calling to preach God's Holy Word to the people and to put into their hands the bread of God . . . .

"My brethren, we are all in our several ways, lay readers, priests, bishop - the chosen vessels of his grace. He takes us into his hands, and though we are to be broken yet are we first blessed; blessed is the greatness of the work to which he calls us - 'Give ye them to eat.' Let us support one another and pray for one another, and above all be confident that in his hands we shall be enough; that if we be but faithful he will accomplish his work in us."

Those who supposed that Dr. Mortimer was more of an academic theologian than anything else must have been surprised at the deeply pastoral note of this address. The sermon fully matched the greatness of the occasion and appealed to the deepest spiritual level of everyone present. Civic and University dignitaries, clergy, readers, laymen from the parishes - they all sensed that a great new era in the Diocese was about to begin.

Immediately after the service the Mayor and Mayoress held a reception at the Guildhall, where the Bishop and Mrs. Mortimer were introduced to the leaders of church and city and were given a great welcome.

On June 14th the Bishop held his first Diocesan Conference at the Civic Hall. The Bishop of Crediton welcomed him officially on behalf of the clergy, and Mr. S. Carlisle Davis on behalf of the laity. In reply, Dr. Mortimer said: "I think that no man ever coming into a diocese received the welcome and encouragement that I have. I have been almost embarrassed by the warmth of friendship I have received on almost every side, and frightened by the height of expectation which you seem to expect of me. I hope you will constantly remember me in your prayers, that God may enable me not too terribly to disappoint you."

To be embarrassed by the warmth of friendship was somehow very characteristic of Robert Mortimer! He said much the same when he received such warm acclaim on his 21st. anniversary as Bishop. He knew that he had great gifts but regarded them as talents given by God to use in the service of others. A similar reception awaited him on his first visit to Tiverton on July 21st. Townsfolk lined the streets to welcome him as he came to preach at a Civic Service at St. Peter's Church. Once again he declared himself frightened by the enthusiastic reception: "The very greatness of the welcome I am everywhere receiving is evidence of the greatness of expectation entertained of me, and I do not feel in myself that I can possibly come up to these expectations."

Why was the reception given to the new Bishop so enthusiastic? For it seems that the warmth of the welcome given to Dr. Mortimer was quite unusual, even where Bishops of Exeter were concerned! One factor was undoubtedly the time of the Bishop's appointment. It was thirteen years since his predecessor, Dr. C.E. Curzon, had been enthroned, but to the people it seemed much longer than that. For the War years, with their poignant memories of the air raids in 1942 which destroyed half the centre of the city, had occupied a good part of Dr. Curzon's reign. Even the Cathedral had been quite seriously damaged, with a third of the choir stalls blown to smithereens. For some seven years Cathedral services had all been held in the Nave, the Choir being screened off until the damage could be repaired. One had memories of Bishop Curzon and Dean Carpenter showing the King and Queen over the maimed Cathedral, amidst piles of fallen masonry, in June 1942.

But now all that was past. Even if the Bishop's Throne was not yet back in place the Cathedral repairs were well under way, and the loving care of wood craftsman Mr. Herbert Read had miraculously restored the choir stalls to their pre-war state. Not only this, but the four years since the end of the War had almost seen the end of austerity and depression, and the future seemed filled with a new hope. Just as churchpeople had seen Dr. Curzon as the guardian of the Diocese during the darkest years of war, so they looked on Dr. Mortimer as their hope for the years ahead.

An even more important factor was Dr. Mortimer's personal qualities, which seemed to meet the people's highest expectations. He looked every inch a Bishop, with his tall frame, dignified and commanding presence and almost princely countenance. He was clearly a man of great learning, who possessed the knowledge needed to guide his flock through the adventurous times which seemed to lie ahead. If he was slightly retiring in manner, he had a natural air of authority which bred confidence and trust.

Exeter was used to Bishops of outstanding quality. Lord William Cecil, who had been Bishop of Exeter from 1916-36, was a very absent-minded and rather eccentric figure, who used to ride around on a yellow bicycle with grimy hands and somewhat dishevelled clothes! But the people loved him; his bearded countenance was very striking and he unmistakably possessed some of the greatness always associated with the Marquess of Salisbury's family. Bishop Curzon who succeeded him was not a man of noble birth, nor was he particularly distinguished as a scholar. He was a parish priest, who had spent years in parishes in Sheffield, Goole and elsewhere, before becoming Bishop of Stepney and then Bishop of Exeter. He was not especially gifted as a preacher. Yet he had an air of gravity and authority about him, such that he easily held his position as Bishop, even when viewed against the exceedingly gracious and scholarly Dean of Exeter, Dr. Carpenter. So Exeter had come to expect great things of its Bishop, and there was an instinctive feeling that Robert Mortimer measured up to its requirements.

One of the Mortimers' first problems was to find a suitable home. There was the Bishop's Palace next to the Cathedral, with its picturesque red stone exterior, albeit uncomfortable and poorly-planned within. This had been built originally by Bishop Briwere in the 13th century, being then one of several residences of the Bishop in different parts of Devon. Since then it had undergone many alterations and had virtually been rebuilt in Victorian Gothic by Ewan Christian about 1846 in Bishop Phillpott's time. The Bishops of Exeter had continued to live in the Palace until the advent of Lord William Cecil, who in spite of his own noble upbringing refused to live there. "My own view," he stated, "is that such a tenancy by bishops is incompatible with their office and against present day feeling. Other people are giving up their homes, and for the bishops to continue living in their palaces seems to invite criticism and misunderstanding."

So he had allowed the Palace to be used as a hospital for the wounded during World War I. Later it became the regional headquarters of the Ministry of Pensions, as it was when Dr. Mortimer arrived. Dr. Curzon, like Bishop Cecil, had first rented a house in Exeter, but he had finally moved to a flat in Pennsylvania Road which was far too small for the Mortimers with their four children. The house which the Diocese had in mind for Dr. Mortimer in 1949 was likewise too small.

So on Dr. Mortimer's arrival in Exeter, his wife and family remained in their Canon's house at Christ Church, the Bishop himself living with the Rev. Sir Patrick Ferguson-Davie, Bt. at the latter's family seat at Creedy, near Crediton. It was not until November 1949 that a temporary home for the Mortimers was at last made ready for them at Peterhayes, Pinhoe, some two miles from the city, where they were to live for four years.

As regards the long term the Bishop expressed a desire to live in the Palace. This was entirely acceptable to the conservative Devonians, many of whom rejoiced in the idea of Dr. Mortimer residing in the house where the Bishops of Exeter had lived on and off for 700 years, where William Temple had been born in 1881 during his father's tenure of the See. At the same time some may have felt it a strange step to take at the onset of a more democratic age! For Dr. Mortimer, however, it seemed the natural thing to do. In the first place he welcomed the chance to live next door to the Cathedral and to enter it through the historic Bishop Oldham corridor (without having to step outside) each time he celebrated the Holy Communion in St. Gabriel's Chapel - as he did every morning when his diary allowed -- or to say his private devotions. Secondly, however, in the words of Professor G.R. Dunstan, "Robert Mortimer was a pontiff cast in an historic mould, the more memorable and more endearing for being, perhaps, the last." Without any sense of pride or affectation Mortimer was a natural prelate who felt that the Palace was the right place for him to live.

It was not until October 1953 that, the repairs and improvements having been completed, the Mortimers were able to move in. It was a costly job to restore the Palace, but none of the expense fell on the Diocese. The Pilgrim Trust provided £20,000 for the express purpose of providing a worthy home for the Cathedral Library, which henceforth was housed at the Palace. The Dean and Chapter contributed £5,000 and the rest of the cost was provided by the Church Commissioners, from a special fund raised by the pooling of the English Episcopal endowments.

The result, under architect Stephen Dykes-Bower, was splendid. Only about half the Palace became the Bishop's home; the other half, which had a separate entrance, included a magnificent gallery for the Cathedral Library, a sizeable Board Room for Diocesan Committees and a number of offices including the Bishop's own office. The Diocesan Board of Finance, which was previously at the Palace Gatehouse, agreed to move into the new offices, though this did not happen until February 1955. The Bishop gave the old Palace Chapel to the Dean and Chapter for conversion into a sacristy and vestry for the Cathedral; in return St. Gabriel's Chapel in the Cathedral was set apart for the Bishop's use. The whole arrangement, which apart from minor changes remains to-day, greatly facilitated Diocesan administration.

To return to June 1949, however, with the Bishop living at Creedy and working from the old office in the Palace, one of Dr. Mortimer's first tasks was to find a successor to Miss Parkhouse, who had been Bishop's Secretary for many years and had just obtained a post with the Church Commissioners. The Bishop appointed his own niece, Miss Mary Fookes, who remained Bishop's secretary for the whole of Dr. Mortimer's twenty-four years at Exeter and continues to work for his successor. When Dr. Mortimer retired he mentioned "my niece-secretary" as one of the two or three people who had given him most help during his episcopate. Her loyal and untiring support, coupled with the experience she gained over the years, was of immense value to him. At the outset, in July 1949, the

Bishop wrote, with characteristic modesty: "The vacuum she (Miss Parkhouse) has left in the Palace is proving very hard to fill. The attempt to fill it is being made by my niece, Miss Fookes. Before long, I am confident, she will rival Miss Parkhouse, but at the moment the pair of us stumble blindly through the intricacies of diocesan administration and try to make as few mistakes as possible."

Dr. Mortimer's arrival in the Diocese brought about no spectacular changes, for his outlook was essentially conservative despite his sympathetic and flexible attitude towards modern needs. It is fair to say that he had no "blueprint" or pre-determined plan of action to lead his Diocese to greater things, and there was no landslide of "advance" within months of his arrival. Rather he sought to improve the quality of church life and worship in every possible way. The earliest sign of his influence, perhaps, was to be seen in the tone of his monthly articles in the *Exeter Diocesan Leaflet*. The first, in August 1949, was on "The Spiritual Discipline of the Laity", being the title of a Report presented to the Church Assembly in 1948. It was followed by articles on each of the six Rules of Life in the Report, e.g. To communicate regularly and at least at Christmas, Easter and Whitsun; To mark by special acts of discipline, Fridays and the Season of Lent; To contribute fairly to the expenses of the Church and to give generously to the needs of others; To keep the Church's marriage laws. In this way the Bishop was laying down, from the first, firm and authoritative moral guidance for his flock.

It is said that he looked and spoke like a man of authority. He often wrote in the language of authority, e.g. "No clergyman or layman may be invited to take the Services (when the incumbent was on holiday) without prior reference to me, unless they already hold my licence," (July 1950). Regarding attendance at the Clergy School in July 1951 the Bishop wrote: "I attach great importance to the attendance of the clergy at the School - particularly of the country clergy . . . . Those who were ordained at or after Trinity 1949 are ordered to attend." Such instructions were more frequent in the early part of Dr. Mortimer's episcopate, but they continued to the end.

In some circumstances such phrasing might have evoked opposition, but by and large the Exeter clergy and laity were ready to accept the Bishop's authority. Somehow he looked the part, and time was soon to show the wisdom of his judgements. Devonians are a little old-fashioned in their ways and a wise, benevolent authority gave them a sense of security.

The first new Diocesan organisation to be mentioned in the *Diocesan Leaflet* was the Clergy Golfing Society! "All my life I have been a great believer in the recreative value of ball-games," the Bishop wrote in his first issue of the *Leaflet* (July 1949), "not only, or even so much, physically, as for the opportunities they give of making friendships." Bristol and Bath and Wells Dioceses already had such a society and Prebendary Shelmerdine was willing to organise one for Exeter. The Bishop gave the venture his full support.

Thanking everyone for their warm-hearted welcome, the Bishop ended his column in this issue of the *Leaflet*: "It is with perfect confidence that we look forward to years of happiness here in Devon." Prophetic indeed these words proved to be. So long, so crammed with events, was Dr. Mortimer's twenty-four year reign that it would not be possible to tackle it chronologically in a book of this length. Rather we review the main features of the episcopate, chapter by chapter, and endeavour to paint a picture of the vast contribution made by Robert Mortimer to the life and learning of the Church.

CHAPTER VIII

Bishop and Pastor

Mr. Arthur Derrick, writing about Dr. Mortimer in the St. Mary Redcliffe Magazine in 1976 noted: "He enjoyed the years at Redcliffe, where he learned the discipline of devotion which he followed faithfully throughout the years at Christ Church and later at Exeter." This was not the first time, in fact, that such a comment had been made - much the same was said of the Bishop while he was a student at Wells. In later years he greatly valued Exeter Cathedral as a house of prayer, and above all his privilege of celebrating the Holy Communion in St. Gabriel's Chapel. Besides celebrating and saying his devotions there, he would often walk around the Cathedral quietly, making its spiritual depths part of himself.

Throughout his busy life the Bishop always set apart times for prayer and devotion. In one corner of his study at The Old Rectory, Newton Reigny, where he lived during retirement, was his prie-dieu. On this simple prayer desk were the Bishop's devotional books, just as he left them before he died. In the centre was the Wells Theological College Office Book. Besides the usual Anglican services it contained Prime, Compline and the monastic hour services of Terce, Sext and None. Well-attuned to the pattern of Catholic Anglican devotion, the Bishop had used these services, day by day, for his private worship. Also on the prie-dieu were the New Testament in Greek, an Office Book with the Mattins and Evensong Lessons already found, and a copy of the Spiritual Letters of the saintly Bishop King.

With such a background the Bishop was always most impressive in church, whether at a magnificent Cathedral service or when preaching at some tiny village church on the moors. "He had the mystique of a Bishop," as Canon Rice described it, and nowhere was this quality more evident than when he was taking part in church worship. At Confirmations and Institutions it was his rule that the Bishop (whether himself or one of his Suffragans) on arrival at the church should be taken straight to the Lady Chapel, where he would remain, either at the prayer desk or in quiet thought, until the service was due to begin. To some incumbents this may have seemed less friendly than to have come to the vestry and spent the time chatting to the clergy, churchwardens and choir. But the custom gave weight to the Bishop's presence and added much to the devotion and dignity of the service. Dr. Mortimer's ascetic appearance and manner perfectly set the tone for every such occasion.

A Bishop's care of his clergy commences with ordinands. In choosing men to be ordained Dr. Mortimer, like all Bishops since the Second World War, was largely guided by the advice of A.C.C.M. Selection Conferences. Very occasionally he disagreed with the Selectors and accepted for training and subsequent ordination a man not recommended by them; rarely, if ever, did he refuse an ordinand who **was** recommended by the Selectors. Like Archbishop William Temple, who shared with him a kindly nature and a strong academic background, Bishop Mortimer was generous in his choice of men for the ministry and not unduly demanding in his requirements. While he liked to have some highly qualified graduates in leading positions, he always gave full scope to those who had not had a university education. He recognised that a priest whose heart was in the right place and who possessed a warm personality with a gift for getting on with others could often do a splendid job in a parish without the need for a great deal of formal theological training. In a few cases he ordained older men with little or no residential training, to the chagrin of the central authorities. On the whole, however, his policy worked out very well.

The list of books in the *Diocesan Directory* to be read by the newly-ordained showed that the Bishop's ideas on the nature of the priesthood were Catholic and traditional. The books included such works as *Ministerial Priesthood* by R.C. Moberly, *Christian Priesthood* by Canon Balmforth and *The Elements of Moral Theology* by the Bishop himself. Some may have felt that they scarcely represented the modern trend, but the books contained very sound teaching, much of which was timeless in its character.

Ordinations by Dr. Mortimer were most solemn and

meaningful occasions, which were never forgotten by those ordained. It so happened that the day before the Bishop died a priest ordained by him at Michaelmas 1951 wrote to him asking for the Bishop's prayers as the priest approached the silver jubilee of his ordination. The priest had only served two years in Exeter Diocese and had then moved elsewhere. But he remembered his ordination with great gratitude and assured the Bishop that he had "never forgotten + Robertus Exon:." He added that he had jotted down in his prayer book some sentences from the Bishop's Charge before the Ordination "which have remained with me - and have not been without effect." Another young priest, himself called John, remembered vividly Dr. Mortimer's Charge based on the words "There was a man sent from God, whose name was John."

Ordination retreats were always held at the Retreat House, Posbury near Crediton, staffed by Sisters of the Franciscan Order of Jesus and Mary. They were unusually long, lasting from Tuesday until Sunday morning. From Tuesday until Friday the Retreat was conducted by the priest appointed, in the traditional manner, with long periods of silence. On the Friday evening the Bishop came to give his Charge to the candidates. These Charges were masterly; they concerned the deepest spiritual aspects of the priest's office and were remembered for years afterwards. Saturday was a fairly free day when the candidates travelled to Exeter to take their official oaths and make other final arrangements.

The Ordination itself took place at 10 a.m. on the Sunday morning, nearly always in the Cathedral. Soon after his arrival, Dr. Mortimer re-ordered the whole service. He celebrated at the nave altar, facing westwards, the Bishop's Chair being placed behind this altar and just in front of the Choir Screen. The Choir themselves sat at the sides, between the Bishop's Chair and the altar, in the nave choir stalls. When the time came for the Bishop to put the official questions to the candidates he moved into the Bishop's Chair and the candidates all moved behind the altar to form a semi-circle before him. It was in this position, too, that the Bishop, with the priests assistant, carried out the ceremony of the laying-on of

hands as, one by one, the candidates knelt before him.
Sometimes the priest-candidates were vested in chasubles
and the deacons in dalmatics, but this was only possible
when a small number was being ordained. The Cathedral
formed a glorious setting for this all-important moment in
the candidates' lives. The Bishop, vested in mitre and
Eucharistic vestments, looked a magnificent figure and he
himself set the tone for this splendid and awesome
occasion. The Bishop somehow developed a strong spiritual
connection with those whom he ordained; they always
looked upon him as truly their Father-in-God and returned
to him for help or advice in times of difficulty.

On Trinity Sunday, June 5th 1955, the Bishop presided
at the first Ordination ever to be televised. It was at the
Cathedral and the Abbot of Nashdom was the preacher.
The broadcast, which was well-received, managed to
convey a great deal of beauty and solemnity of the Exeter
Ordination rite.

Until 1961 the Diocesan Missioner had also been the
Director of Ordination Training, the two offices being held
by Prebendary W.A.P. Dawson and from 1955-61 by the
Rev. Henry Kendall. In 1961, however, the Bishop asked
Canon F.G. Rice, who was the Vicar of St. David's, Exeter
and was already Honorary Chaplain to Dr. Mortimer, to
take the smaller parish of St. Mary Arches and to become
both Domestic Chaplain to the Bishop and Director of
Ordination Training. As regards the care of the ordinands,
the Bishop, very characteristically, said to Fr. Rice at the
time: "I am a good theorist but I don't know how to deal
with the chaps - you do that." Canon Rice remained in
office for the whole of the Bishop's time and afterwards;
during these years a very adequate supply of ordinands
offered themselves for ordination in the Diocese.

As regards Post-Ordination Training the Diocese has
never been able to provide a comprehensive system of
part-time tuition such as the more compact dioceses, like
Manchester, lay on. But in Devon the geographical
difficulties are acute - the area of the county is very
large, the parishes are scattered and at least four different
centres would be needed if regular classes were held which
were reasonably accessible to all the junior clergy.

Dr. Mortimer did however continue the Annual Clergy School started by Bishop Curzon which was held at St. Luke's College, Exeter for four days each July. The School was open to all diocesan clergy, who could either be resident or attend as "day-boys". Clergy were obliged to attend for their first three years in Orders.

Dr. Mortimer, with his very wide circle of contacts, was able to secure absolutely first-rate speakers for this event. Over the years they included Archbishops Fisher and Ramsey, Bishop J.W.C. Wand, Mr. C.S. Lewis, Sir Hugh Trevor-Roper, Professor John Macquarrie and others of similar calibre. Some sixty clergy attended each year and there was a real infusion of fresh ideas into the minds of the clergy. There was also a one-day conference for the newly-ordained held at the Bishop's Palace in November or December each year, usually with a single visiting speaker. During his first three years in Orders each priest or deacon would be allocated a tutor - usually a parish priest with an academic bent - living not too far away who would supervise his studies. There were also one or two groups of junior clergy who met about once a month under a tutor, studying the New Testament in Greek and discussing important areas of theology.

In 1956 the Bishop appointed Canon Henry Balmforth as Chancellor of the Cathedral following Canon McLaren's retirement. An elderly erudite priest of traditional Catholic views, he had previously been Principal of Ely Theological College, and he shared with Canon Rice the supervision of the Post-Ordination Training. A useful addition to the staff, he retired in 1973, to be succeeded by the Chaplain of Exeter University, the Rev. J.A. Thurmer. Canon Thurmer, who had earlier been Chaplain of Salisbury Theological College, was well qualified to supervise Post-Ordination Training, but he had only been in office a few months when the Bishop retired.

From time to time one-day Conferences were held for the clergy on topics like the Hospital Chaplain's Work and the Sacrament of Penance. Courses with regular monthly meetings were arranged on various subjects; one of these held in 1972 involved twelve sessions in Exeter on the problems of Marriage, Separation and Divorce designed to give clergy expert knowledge in this field. It was later repeated in Barnstaple. Retreats for the clergy, laity and special groups were regularly held at the Retreat House, Posbury. The Bishop did all he could to ensure that expert instruction was available to clergy in every branch of their work.

Dr. Mortimer had a great personal concern for the welfare of his clergy and as Bishop Westall has testified, "his handling of their problems was astonishingly wise." An Archdeacon records that when a particular priest was suggested at a staff meeting to fill a vacant benefice, the Bishop would say, "Oh no! That wouldn't do. He has three boys at school. Education would be very difficult" - when other members of the staff had not even realised the problem. Another Archdeacon recalled a time when he set off, firmly determined to deal with a priest who had caused the Bishop great hurt and embarrassment. "Be gentle with him," the Bishop pleaded, "be gentle with him." The lasting impression of Dr. Mortimer, this Archdeacon wrote, was not of a head but of a heart.

Because of his intellectual acumen, in fact, the Bishop knew far more about individual clergy and their parishes than most of them ever realised, and in dealing with clergy in trouble he brought a keen mind and a loving heart. "If only people would come to me sooner I could help them so much more," Dr. Mortimer would say with a sigh to his Chaplain, "but now there is a well-nigh hopeless situation."

Within the Diocese the Bishop was well-known for the special pains he took to restore to a useful ministry priests who had run into serious trouble at some stage of their career. He would place them, incognito as it were, in a parish far from the district where they had previously served, and do all possible to help them on their feet again. One of the clergy thus assisted was an Archdeacon from a distant diocese; the Bishop would help in this way both his own clergy and those passed on to him by other Diocesans. Owing to the highly confidential nature of this work it is difficult to mention examples and it is not easy even for the author to obtain a full picture. Our general impression is that there were more failures than successes in this part of the Bishop's work. Despite the Christian hope to the contrary, it seems hard in practice for the leopard to change his spots! But there were instances where a priest who had lost all hope was restored to a useful sphere of service, thanks to the Bishop's concern.

The Bishop believed in long incumbencies, and some clergy did not think he was quite so understanding when they wanted to move before he thought they should! Once after instituting a vicar he was heard to say to the local mayor, "Well, I've put him in and I hope not to hear a cheep from him for another twenty years." A curate who arranged to see the Bishop, hoping for an early move, said, "Robert looked at me as if I was a basket of adders!"

Every Bishop has to deal with a stream of complaints from parishioners about their incumbents. Some complaints border on the frivolous, of course, but inevitably there were a few priests in the Diocese who merited the adverse comments which arrived at the Palace by the morning post. In replying to such letters the Bishop would always back up his clergy as far as he possibly could. In certain cases the priest would receive a firm, if kindly, note of censure from the Bishop but Dr. Mortimer would never, except in quite indefensible cases, admit to the complainant that the parish priest was seriously at fault. The Bishop's loyalty to his clergy in such circumstances greatly strengthened their loyalty to him.

The Bishop showed the same pastoral concern for laymen who sought his advice. Many of these, of course, were parties involved in divorce and remarriage. Dr. Mortimer's reverence for the sanctity of marriage prevented his consenting to a second marriage in church in such cases, which in any case was forbidden by Convocation rules, nor would he agree to a quasi-"wedding" in church after a Register Office ceremony where divorce was concerned. Prayers for the happiness of the second marriage could be said in church, but only the priest and the couple could be present and the Bishop was unhappy about the word "blessing" being used. In accordance with Convocation regulations he would ask such couples not to receive Holy Communion for a short period, say three months, but never permanently excommunicated them. He always had the greatest sympathy for people in this predicament, and the surprising lengths to which he went in supporting legislation for easier divorce arose largely from his unhappiness at seeing so many couples being forced to "live in sin".

The Bishop loved ministering to individuals, rarely as the chance came to him on his episcopal round. Once, despite the counter-attractions of sport, he went out on a Saturday afternoon to a village twenty miles away to confirm a candidate suffering from multiple sclerosis who was unable to leave her home. On his departure after the service he said to the incumbent, "What a lovely way to spend a Saturday afternoon!"

On another occasion a tiny little girl, who had been allowed as a special treat to go to Evensong at the local church to see the Bishop, who was preaching, stepped out of her pew as Dr. Mortimer was passing in the Procession, stood in front of the Bishop and firmly blocked his way! He looked at her, smiled and blessed her with the sign of the Cross. He then bent down and said to her, "Now you have seen me, go back to your mother." Very quietly she returned at once to the pew.

While he always reverenced the Catholic tradition in which he had grown up, Dr. Mortimer was broad-minded in his churchmanship and never liked to be regarded as a separatist. In a sermon at an Anglo-Catholic function the Bishop once said, "The word Anglo-Catholic is one of which I have never been fond. I am, after the flesh, an Englishman; and by grace a member of the Catholic Church. I am, therefore, in common with all members of the Church of England, an English Catholic." Bishop Thomas Bloomer, an Evangelical with whom Dr. Mortimer had numerous discussions in his closing years, wrote: "We had many meetings together, usually in opposite camps, yet always growing in friendliness and understanding." Even so, the Bishop was quite happy to read a paper on The Sacraments to the Anglo-Catholic Congress. He was always willing to take a Confirmation in rochet and chimere, abandoning his cope and mitre, if politely asked to do so by the incumbent; though there were very few parishes in the Diocese, especially during later years, where such a request would be made. Dr. Mortimer did not like "strongholds" where an extreme type of churchmanship prevailed at all the churches in the area, and would try to break them up by ensuring that incumbents of more moderate views were appointed when vacancies arose.

When the Billy Graham Crusades reached their peak in 1954 and 1955 Dr. Mortimer surprised the Anglo-Catholics by speaking out in their favour. "In spite of the 'fundamentalist' theology which appears to underlie Dr. Graham's conception of the Christian religion," the Bishop wrote in April 1955, "it is my belief that Dr. Graham has a remarkable power of confronting or reconfronting the individual with the challenge of our Lord -- 'Come, follow me'. It is also Dr. Graham's continually asserted conviction that the Christian life can only be lived in association with the Christian family at worship. ... I can see no objection to these meetings being relayed into our parish churches. Two of them are to be relayed into the Cathedral and on these occasions the Bishop of Plymouth and I shall take the chair." Dr. Mortimer realised the strong position of Evangelicals, in fact. They preached a clear message, which was often lacking from other sections of the Church. The Bishop hoped that all clergy receiving enquirers' cards sent in at these Crusades would receive them sympathetically. "This is not to be regarded as a momentary lapse into emotionalism. It indicates some need. It is for the parish priest to find out what, and to meet it."

As an 'English Catholic' Dr. Mortimer was often supposed to be very keen on ceremonial in worship. Certainly he had a great sense of history and tradition, and from this point of view he valued ceremonial which was on an ancient Christian pattern. On St. Peter's Day 1953 in the Cathedral he wore a pair of episcopal gloves which had belonged to Jonathan Trelawney, Bishop of Exeter from 1689-1708. He wrote: "I must confess to a certain thrill in wearing something owned and used by a famous predecessor of over 200 years ago. The wearing of ceremonial gloves by bishops on great occasions is now unusual, but it has never been wholly discontinued by the Church of England. ... Like the gloves which the Queen wore at her Coronation, they are a symbol of authority."

At the same time the Bishop's lack of fussiness tended to produce in him a certain dislike of ceremonial, or at any rate he liked it to be as simple as possible. When his great friend Dr. Kirk became Bishop of Oxford the latter appointed the then Principal of St. Stephen's House, the Rev. A.H. Couratin, as his Honorary Chaplain in matters ceremonial. Whenever Dr. Kirk held an Ordination in Christ Church Cathedral, for example, Fr. Couratin took charge and arranged all the ritual. On being appointed Bishop of Exeter, Dr. Mortimer invited Fr. Couratin, whom he knew well, to design his first mitre and certain other robes. The mitre, which was of a tall and very dignified shape, was made by the Clewer Sisters; Canon Couratin understands that the design came originally from a figure of a Bishop (perhaps Wykeham or Waynflete!) in one of the chantries of Winchester Cathedral.

On his arrival in Exeter Dr. Mortimer, following Dr. Kirk's example, appointed the Rev. Sir Patrick Ferguson-Davie, Bt., at whose Creedy Park home the Bishop stayed for his first few months in the Diocese, as his Chaplain for matters of ceremonial. Sir Patrick and Fr. Couratin were frequently in touch over ceremonial questions and became friends; Fr. Couratin often stayed at Creedy. Bishop Mortimer decided that there should be an official Episcopal Use in Exeter Diocese, to which all parishes should conform. This avoided the Bishop having to find out a hundred and one different parochial Uses! Following Fr. Couratin the Bishop worked on the principle that nothing should be done which did not have to be done, but where ceremonial was indicated it should be done in the most dignified manner.

Sir Patrick became an assiduous **caeremonarius** and in 1961 he published a book, *The Bishop in Church,* which set out the approved ritual and was profusely illustrated with photographs. The Bishop wrote a Foreword, part of which runs "I handed the whole business (of ceremonial) over to Sir Patrick Ferguson-Davie. This book describes more or less the result. I am deeply grateful to Sir Patrick for the vast amount of trouble and irritation he has saved me. And I greatly admire the skill and devotion which he has brought. . . . There is generally a complete absence of fuss and bother and confusion. . . . Not that we always do everything as described in this book. Sometimes we forget and sometimes we disobey on principle. By and large we all conform."

This book is unique among modern Church of England works, and must have been a help in other dioceses. For some time it was used at Cathedral Ordinations and Sir Patrick would be in charge of ceremonial. As the Bishop pointed out it was not always enforced, either in Cathedral or parish church, but for over ten years it provided the pattern.

Preaching is a vital part of the Christian ministry, and Dr. Mortimer took his responsibilities in this direction very seriously. Most of his sermons were typed out in full and all were very carefully prepared. The Bishop never succumbed to a popular type of Catholicism which says that the Sacraments are so important that sermons - the Ministry of the Word - do not matter. Nor did he subscribe to another popular idea - that the day of the sermon was over. "One of his greatest gifts," wrote the Ven. A.F. Ward, "was to be able to express the great facts of the Faith in the simplest way. I see him at an Institution, sitting on the episcopal chair at the entry to the choir, talking to his people - a real Father-in-God - in words which everyone could understand, and making the Faith live." Even more masterly, perhaps, were the Bishop's six-minute sermons at the Cathedral on the Great Festivals, in which he had an amazing knack of communicating, as it seemed, all that mattered about the Incarnation, or the Resurrection, or the Coming of the Holy Spirit, in this very short space of time. His Confirmation addresses may not have seemed quite "with it" to the modern teenage generation, especially in later years. They had a ring of seriousness which is not quite in fashion at the present time. But even so excellent teaching was given and the candidate was made to feel that Confirmation was a momentous event in his life.

At the Mothers' Union Triennial Festival at the Cathedral in July 1969 the Bishop emphasised in his sermon that it was not a Wives' Union but a **Mothers'** Union. The all-important thing was that members should bring up their children as good churchmen - a difficult task in modern times but one that was immensely worthwhile. At a service for Accountants the Bishop took as his text 1 Cor 52, "Moreover it is required in stewards that a man be found faithful." How frail and vulnerable was professional honour! If they refrained from doing wrong merely from fear of the consequences if they were found out, their professional standards would not last a generation! Their rule must be: "I certify only what I know to be right and above board; nothing will induce me to do otherwise." Dr. Mortimer's opening addresses at the Diocesan Conference were always of high quality and sometimes brilliant - over the years he covered a very wide variety of subjects and the addresses were invariably relevant to modern life.

Lack of space unfortunately prevents our describing many other aspects of the Bishop's teaching. Much of his advice is summed up in the Visitation Charges which he gave his clergy in 1952 and 1956, the latter coming after the Synod of all the clergy which he held in 1955. The priest should not be "submerged" by parochial chores - it was vital that he had time, not only for devotion but for serious reading. A priest was an apostle sent from God and "unless we abide in Him we can do nothing." The Bishop was worried by the shortage of clergy, little realising that there would be far fewer in 1978! He stressed the need to improve their stipends, which happily are far better in 1978 than in 1952. The laity owed it to the priest to free him from constant worry over lack of money. The Bishop laid great stress (much less fashionable as it was in 1956 than to-day) on Holy Communion being **the** act of the Church's worship on Sundays and Holy Days. Dr. Mortimer was very worried about the growing practice of 'indiscriminate Baptism', even though to him it was unthinkable that the children of Christian parents should not be baptised in infancy. Much more careful parental preparation was needed before infant Baptism. He emphasised the value of sacramental Confession as a means of forgiveness of sins. As regards the "growing practice" of cremation, this need cause no anxiety. It did not conflict with belief in the Resurrection of the Body, but there should always be a service in church first. Clearly the attitude to cremation has greatly changed since those days! Much of Dr. Mortimer's advice, however, is still of value to-day.

CHAPTER IX

Robert Mortimer - The Man

It is often said of a person: "It is not what he did, but what he was." Robert Mortimer undertook a vast number of works in his lifetime, many beneficial to Church and people, but he will be remembered most for what he was. We have already mentioned his natural elegance. "He might well have stepped from a medieval window - a Grandisson or a Bronescombe come alive and among us," Canon Rice wrote, the two named being early Bishops of Exeter who were great Cathedral builders. Bishop Westall expressed a similar idea in different words: "He looked and spoke as a man of authority.... I think he would have been at home in the 18th century if the Oxford Movement had started in 1733 instead of 1833." Yet Dr. Mortimer was intensely alive to modern human problems and his presence carried authority in the 20th century just as it might have done in the 18th.

The second point about the Bishop to strike one forcibly was the extreme agility of his mind. "I always envied Bob his wonderful ability to join in a debate with an impromptu speech which always cleared the air and often brought the matter to a sensible conclusion at once," wrote Dr. H.J. Carpenter, formerly Bishop of Oxford. Dr. Mortimer's special intellectual gift was one often associated with brilliant lawyers - the ability to penetrate rapidly through masses of details to the heart of the matter, to see clearly the point at issue which so often eluded others. The Diocesan Registrar, Mr. J.F.G. Michelmore wrote: "I have always admired.... the speed and incisiveness with which he solved so many problems, so that in many cases few people realised that they ever existed. It was only after he left the Diocese that a wider circle came to appreciate the skill with which he concentrated other people's thought on the task in hand and avoided digression."

One consequence of this was the Bishop's tendency to deal with complex personal problems almost immediately in many cases, rather than ponder over them for some time. To lengthy letters setting out a difficult and involved situation Dr. Mortimer often replied by return of post with a letter of three or four lines giving the perfect solution to the problem. Brother Denis, S.S.F. remembers how the Bishop once answered a letter of several pages with a postcard bearing the words: "Why not? + R.E.!" Mr. P.B.M. Savage, formerly Headmaster of Summer Fields, Oxford, wrote: "In whatever capacity he was writing, his letters were little masterpieces. They usually ran to about three lines and were signed '+ Bob'. In that small space they somehow managed to say all that was needed without appearing at all brusque or unfriendly." It was inevitable, of course, that some would suspect that these short letters implied a lack of concern, but here they would have been entirely wrong. The Bishop's brilliant mind had seen the answer in a flash, and he had written it down in the shortest possible space.

Dr. Mortimer's ability to 'see through the trees' and size up a situation applied just as much to wider issues of diocesan policy as to personal problems, though he could not solve every difficulty in a matter of minutes! We quote Canon Rice again: "He spent much anxious time and thought on difficult and controversial questions, but once his mind was made up he was quite fearless and never showed the least sign of faltering. 'It is going to be mighty difficult this time but I must tackle it, as the (Diocesan) Conference is expecting it. It won't go down too well, some of them will howl at me for it - but in six months' time I believe they will see I was right'." Often both clergy and laity would say later on: "Of course the Bishop was right. Why didn't we think of it ourselves?"

As Bishop Westall wrote, Robert Mortimer was never devious. It is often claimed that a parish priest must be devious to some extent to do his job successfully. Even St. Paul was "all things to all men", and many a churchman has used these words as a pretext for preaching "smooth things" in a tricky situation. But the Bishop did not have it in him to be devious - he had a great reverence for the truth and some of his colleagues found him almost childlike in his honesty. As Canon Rice put it, far from playing to the gallery, as so many Church leaders are tempted to do to-day, Dr. Mortimer did not seem to be aware that there was a gallery! As Bishop Sanderson wrote; Robert Mortimer showed "an inability to wear a mask or be anything but himself." Many had cause to be thankful to the Bishop for the very high ethical standards which he maintained in Diocesan affairs.

The Bishop had a great sense of humour and amongst friends could be hilariously amusing. Sometimes his humour even intruded into official correspondence. When he became Bishop the College of Arms approved a beautiful Coat-of-Arms for him, in which the Arms of the See of Exeter impaled those of his family. The latter included, quarterly, the Arms of the ancient Earls of March as we have explained. In 1954 an old wag from near Tiverton wrote him a stern letter declaring that he had no right to use the Arms of the Earls of March - surely, as a Christian leader, he should show propriety in such matters! The Bishop replied:

"I am myself, of course, totally ignorant of even the first principles of heraldry. In my ignorance, or innocence, I have always supposed that the last word with these matters lay with the College of Heralds. And what am I to do? I cannot invent a Coat of Arms for myself, surely? Can I do other than display the Coat of Arms authorised by the College of Heralds?

The March blood may or may not run in my veins. It has always been assumed that it does, though the evidence is as thin, or thinner, than the blood must now be. Part of the evidence, if I have understood the thing right, is the very fact of the grant of this Coat of Arms by the College of Heralds in, I think, the 18th century. But now I find that to you this grant is actually evidence against the assumption, rather than in favour of it (the correspondent had suggested that these ancient Arms had only been granted to Dr. Mortimer as a mark of respect for his position as Bishop of Exeter!). However, my eldest brother knows a great deal more about this than I do, and I have sent your letter on to him."

The number of anecdotes told about the Bishop is phenomenal and most of the stories are far from apocryphal - they really happened! A great many concern the Bishop's passion for sport or his mild weakness for gin and tonic which latterly somewhat superseded his glass of port. One heard of a Confirmation at a remote village in North Devon, reached by the Bishop after a long drive in wintry weather. The service completed, a churchwarden invited the Bishop home to a glass of Horlick's. The Bishop's reply in this case truly was apocryphal!

Another time the Bishop was due to confirm some Cathedral choirboys on a Saturday afternoon. It was a task that normally delighted him, but this time he was sad. "It's the European Cup Final on Saturday afternoon!" he bemoaned, "What bad staff work!" Then an impish glint came into his blue eyes. "Do you think we could arrange to have a small TV set in the Throne?" His Chaplain doubted whether this could be done. Persisting in his quiet humour, however, the Bishop said: "I think we might get the Head Virger to put the score up - England on the hymn board and West Germany on the psalm board." In the end he made the best of the situation by giving an address which was as brilliant as it was brief and returning to the Palace in time to see the second half of the match on TV.

Another Saturday afternoon he was on his way to an Institution with one of his Archdeacons, but he was not in the best of moods! This was because the England v. Scotland Rugby International was on that afternoon. However after the service, while he and the Archdeacon were on the way to their car, he looked through a cottage window and saw the match in full swing on the TV. He knocked on the door and, receiving no reply, he tried the door which was unlocked. "Are you coming?" the Bishop said. "No," said the Archdeacon, "I'll wait to see if you get thrown out!" With that the Bishop went in and soon reappeared at the door to call the Archdeacon. The man in the house, who was sat glued to the set, was stone deaf - that was why there had been no reply! So the two clerics made gestures to him, drew up chairs in front of the TV and watched the match until the end, the Bishop in purple and the Archdeacon in scarlet! At the end the two ecclesiastics waved their thanks to the old man and left. "I often wondered what the poor chap thought," the Archdeacon said afterwards! One of the Bishop's greatest pleasures at home, in fact, was with a glass in his hand to watch cricket, rugger, tennis, golf or soccer on TV. While for some years after the War the Mortimers had no television set, the Bishop later learned to amend his ways!

Yet another time the Bishop was confirming beyond Crediton and was surprised to see a tawny owl on top of the Choir Screen! Afterwards he asked the Lady of the Manor, who had invited him around for sherry, about this mysterious bird. "Is it alive?" he queried. "Of course not, it's stuffed," replied the lady, who was also a Churchwarden. "Then what is it doing there?" "It's to keep the bats away," she answered. "I've never heard such nonsense - sheer superstition!" the Bishop retorted. Quite undaunted the hostess, who had the measure of her guest, said, "My dear Bishop, I know you are a learned theologian but with respect you are lamentably ignorant of country ways and doings. We were pestered with bats, but since that little owl has been sitting up there we haven't seen a sign of a bat. You can think what you like, but I tell you it passes the pragmatic test. It works. So there! Do have another drink." "Yes Mary," said the Bishop, "that's the best possible answer."

As an administrator Dr. Mortimer was very good indeed. Having that quiet self-assurance which springs naturally from greatness of stature, the Bishop was completely free from fussiness and red tape was reduced to an absolute minimum. There was none of that massive outpouring of duplicated sheets, or preoccupation with fiddling rules and regulations, which lesser men feel are necessary to underline their authority. The Bishop certainly expected things to be well done, particularly where worship was concerned, and he would chide his subordinates if they failed to achieve the necessary standards. But he always showed great trust in those who served him well; typically he would say to a junior colleague: "Well, write a letter to him about it, John. You know what to write - you know what my views are on this matter," rather than insist on knowing exactly what was to be written. In this way he reduced office chores to a bare minimum - his extremely brief letters were an added help! - and so saved time and mental energy for more creative activities. Life at the Bishop's Office was surprisingly informal - clergy and laity could breeze in without ceremony and a very friendly atmosphere prevailed.

As Chairman of Committees Dr. Mortimer was generally ajudged to be excellent, though a few felt that he was too impatient to finish the meeting quickly! Mr. P.M.B. Savage, formerly Headmaster of Summer Fields, the Oxford Preparatory School, describes the Bishop, in his capacity of Chairman of the Governors, thus:

"He used to slope in, with his hands in his pockets, at about twenty nine and a half minutes past two and find us, with emptied coffee cups, waiting. 'Isn't it about time that we got on with this meeting?' he would say; and we followed him in exactly as the clock struck half-past. We were released, equally punctually, yet not feeling in the least rushed, at fifty nine and a half minutes past three in time for tea. Round the table we sat, while Bob, fed with the facts by Johnnie Max-Muller, would, without giving offence or being in the smallest degree pompous, politely let everyone say just what was needed, stop them from rambling and extract the essence, like a bee gathering honey. We thought he had forgotten all about us and our affairs since the last meeting. We were quite wrong."

Dr. Mortimer brought the same gifts as Chairman of Diocesan meetings - he was humorous, swift and decisive. His skills were particularly in evidence at the Diocesan Conference, where it was never easy to transact business with up to a thousand potential speakers present. However the Bishop had a remarkable knack of eliciting useful contributions from those with something worthwhile to say, while tactfully repressing those who would have talked out time to no purpose.

The Bishop's greatest personal handicap was his shyness. A few months before his death Dr. Mortimer told a friend that he had been painfully shy all his life and that this was one of the greatest burdens he had had to face. It seems strange at first sight that a man with an intellect such that he could make rings round most people in discussion or argument should be so restricted. But this is a weakness that some are born with, and in general no amount of determination can overcome it. Furthermore in most cases it is not lightened by increasing age and experience, for the joy and attractivness of youth enable young people to conquer it in a way which is denied to the older man.

As always it affected the Bishop most in particular situations. When preaching, lecturing or debating in the House of Lords he was completely at ease and more than fluent. When speaking to small groups or individuals about serious matters or business affairs he was usually comfortable enough. But he had no small talk and seemed to be altogether ill at ease in informal conversation with those he did not know well. He would then rapidly become bored and sometimes felt an almost compelling desire to leave. The cup of tea in the Church Hall after the service he found especially trying and often arranged for his Archdeacon or Chaplain to "rescue" him a short while after it had started. "Let's slip away as soon as we decently can, I can't bear these sausage rolls!" he would say and often the Bishop and his colleague would enjoy a meal at some hostelry on the way home! He simply did not have the small talk to chat comfortably to the parishioners who were so keen to meet their Father-in-God. This was unfortunate as the Bishop gained a reputation for aloofness or disinterest which was quite undeserved. But there was nothing he could do about it.

Sometimes things would work out differently. In 1973 the Bishop visited St. Saviour's, Dartmouth for its 600th Anniversary. To give a little colour to the occasion it was arranged with the Britannia Royal Naval College that the Bishop should be taken from Brixham to Dartmouth on a minesweeper and meet the clergy, choir and the parish at the landing stage. The sea was rough, the Bishop did not look at all happy about the journey and it was widely rumoured that he would be seasick! When it came to the point, however, while several new recruits were hanging their heads over the rails as the ship rounded the stormy Berry Head, there was the Bishop - fortified by one or two whiskies which always put him more at his ease - the centre of attention in the wardroom! Surrounded by young officers, he was heard to say, "Of course it is very unwise for anyone to read Sociology in a *first* degree at Oxford!" But then, in a sense, the Bishop was talking "shop".

While Dr. Mortimer's shyness could sometimes be a barrier in his personal relationships with clergy and others, those who managed to penetrate his "shell" found him an immensely human, warm and compassionate person. At most Vicarages before the service the Bishop's dignified air instinctively moved the incumbent's children to be on their best behaviour, and in many cases their parents firmly instructed them to this end! But now and again there was a vicar who knew that the Bishop would be very happy to sit on the floor and play with the children if only he were given the chance.

As regards his own family, Dr. Mortimer had been able to spend a good deal of time with them while at Christ Church, but as Bishop of Exeter his heavy programme of evening and week-end engagements, not to mention his long periods away at Convocation, the House of Lords and the like, made it difficult for him to see a lot of his family, especially as the children were away at school for much of the time. Here Mrs. Mortimer did a splendid job, as several of their friends have testified, caring devotedly for their four children while their father was away. But the Bishop was very attached to his family, and among his papers were lovingly preserved scores of letters from the children, often written from school. Written in very natural, affectionate language, they bear witness to a happy and united family.

Dr. Mortimer followed the children's school progress with great interest - the school reports were carefully filed away - and was proud of the fine careers they achieved. He officated at Edward's wedding to Miss Elizabeth Zanetti at the Cathedral on October 5th 1968 -as his future daughter-in-law was a Roman Catholic he was assisted by Fr. N. Coote, a priest of this denomination. The Bishop likewise conducted Katharine's wedding to Mr. John Nicholson, also at the Cathedral, on July 7th 1973; on this occasion Bishop Westall gave a short address. The Mortimers could not attend Sophia's wedding to Mr. Eli Schutts of Brooklyn, U.S.A. on June 14th 1968 as this was in Connecticut, but a letter from a friend gave very full details of the ceremony.

Our last reference must be to the Bishop's leisure activities. The family delighted in entertaining their friends at the Palace and the Bishop spent a fair amount of his spare time acting as host. Some of these friendships went back a great many years. The Bishop loved reading for pleasure, despite the large amount of scholarly and ecclesiastical literature which he had to read as a part of his daily work. He was very keen on the novels of Trollope and, in earlier years, John Galsworthy's works. He enjoyed P.G. Wodehouse and read a good many detective stories, especially those of Dorothy L. Sayers. Over the last five years of his life he became much attached to Mozart's works on gramophone records.

Sport remained a consuming passion. We have referred elsewhere to the Bishop's golfing activities and his annual visit to Lord's for the Varsity match. Although he never became a member of the M.C.C. (as his father-in-law was) he always relished the chance to attend Test Matches or an occasional county game at the venerable ground at St. John's Wood. Equally attractive were Rugby fixtures at Twickenham or tennis at Wimbledon; one year he was given two tickets for the Royal Box at Wimbledon and out of the blue invited a fellow-cleric to go with him. He loved to arrange, and in earlier years to play in, *ad hoc* cricket matches. There was no easier way for a stranger to penetrate his natural reserve than to talk enthusiastically about sport.

Holidays too he greatly enjoyed and several of his friends seem to have remembered most of all the happy times they spent with him on vacation. Bishop H.J. Carpenter, who had known him since the two had attended Mods. lectures together at Oxford, recalled vividly a car holiday in France which they had had as far back as 1937 - "I am afraid I was a rather dull and useless companion, because among other things he had to do all the driving," observed Dr. Carpenter modestly, "but for me it was a most enjoyable expedition." In similar vein Mr. Dick Walters describes a motoring holiday in France and Spain which the pair enjoyed in 1950: "We had decided that our revels should be based on the principle that sightseeing was only a way to fill in time between meals, and that meals themselves were only an excuse for tasting the wine of the country! .... We parted after a very happy holiday without a scratch on the car and never a cross word. The last phrase summed up our friendship for over 50 years."

While the Bishop very frequently went on holiday with his wife and family, he retained to the end a certain taste for "bachelor" holidays of the type described. Perhaps this arose from his long years in all-male colleges. Often he stayed with the Rev. H.E. Kendall, who had a cottage at Mevagissey where not only the Bishop but scores of others connected with St. Edward's School would spend the odd week-end. Informality was the keynote of these holidays and it is related that one Sunday morning the Bishop and Fr. Kendall attended early Communion at Mevagissey Church dressed in open-necked shirts. The congregation was not large and after the service the vicar's wife asked the sidesmen why they had not approached the two visitors at the back. The contemptuous answer was: "Them hikers? They never 'as no money!"

In later years the Bishop also stayed at the Paignton home of Prebendary Gordon Samuel, formerly Vicar of Totnes. Often he was accompanied by Canon Rice. On these occasions the Bishop loved shopping at the Keymarket in Paignton, and walking around the fish market at Brixham. Sometimes the same trio would stay with Fr. Samuel's mother at Bournemouth, or with friends in North Devon. The Bishop was very relaxed at such times - it was as if he divided his life into two separate compartments. On these holidays he was one of a bunch of friends, but when he was Bishop he was Bishop and woe betide any cleric who presumed upon the friendship!

Like many Bishops Dr. Mortimer belonged to the Athenaeum. He was also a member of the lesser-known but none-the-less distinguished circle calling itself "Nobody's Friends", to which he was introduced by Mr. Justice Vaisey. Founded in 1800 as the friends of one William Stevens, it has equal numbers of clergy and laity as members and includes peers, bishops, deans and other Church dignitaries, judges, lawyers and Service officers. Its groundwork is stated to be the Principles of Religion and Polity. Even in his last year, 1976, the Bishop attended their meetings several times.

So Dr. Mortimer, more than many men who hold high office, deliberately set out to find time for social and recreational activities amidst his very busy life. "All work and no play makes Jack a dull boy." To set aside time for leisure activities in this way made life even busier when he did get back to his desk! But these spells of leisure deepened his human contacts and increased his capacity for work; for both him and his friends they were times of much happiness.

CHAPTER X

The Diocese - Officers and Organisations

It is sometimes said that by the time a Bishop has built up the team that he wants for his diocese he is ready to retire! For all beneficed clergy, whether Bishops Suffragan, Archdeacons or leading incumbents, have the freehold - and in Dr. Mortimer's time there was not even an upper age limit! For years after his appointment a Bishop has to work with immediate colleagues most of whom have been chosen by his predecessor.

Dr. Mortimer was more successful than most Diocesans in building up his own team. This was partly because of the length of his episcopate but partly, too, because a good many dignitaries retired during his first few years as Bishop. As early as 1950 the Bishop of Plymouth, the Rt. Rev. F.W. Daukes, retired and the Crown accepted Dr. Mortimer's nomination of Canon N.H. Clarke to succeed him. Canon Clarke had been Vicar of Plymouth since 1945. For a year he was Bishop, Archdeacon and Vicar of Plymouth all at once, as some of his predecessors had been, but Dr. Mortimer did not favour this arrangement and Bishop Clarke resigned the vicarage in 1951. The Bishop described him in 1950 thus: "A man of great intellectual power, he is also a wise pastor of quite indefatigable energy" - high praise indeed! Bishop Clarke was tall and broad, pleasant and gentle in manner, with a firm Evangelical faith. Dr. Mortimer found Bishop Clarke's outgoing manner attractive, and the two bishops got on well together, the Bishop of Exeter often pulling his Suffragan's leg at their difference in churchmanship.

This appointment illustrated two features of Dr. Mortimer's policy in making such choices. Firstly he often appointed men of very different gifts from his own. Bishop Clarke was an Evangelical, Dr. Mortimer a Catholic; the one was rather extrovert the other somewhat introvert. Dr. Mortimer's broadmindedness in this respect much increased the value of his appointments and was a source of great strength to the Diocese.

Secondly, Dr. Mortimer very frequently appointed

clergy from his own diocese to high offices like this. In so doing he encouraged clergy to remain in the Diocese and so gave greater continuity, but there was not so much cross-fertilisation with the outside world. If there was any truth in one Archdeacon's remark: "Devon is fifty years behind London in its thinking on Church matters," this may in part have been the reason, though the Archdeacon in question had spent by far the greatest part of his ministry in Exeter Diocese! Dr. Mortimer felt that he himself provided an adequate contact with the outside world, and like many men of great intellect he tended to be over-charitable in his judgement on the minds of others.

Unlike some Diocesans Dr. Mortimer had no compunction at all about appointing those he knew well, sometimes from earlier days, to important positions. In September 1978, announcing that Canon R.H. Babington, Vicar of St. Mary-le-Tower, Ipswich, was to be Archdeacon of Exeter he added: "Canon Babington was a fellow-student with me at Oxford and at Wells Theological College, so I have known him for a very long time. That sounds bad, and smacks of the eighteenth century! All the same in a very short time the Diocese, the Archdeaconry and the City will find themselves enriched by the presence of Canon and Mrs. Babington among us." The Bishop's words proved true; Archdeacon Babington was well regarded in the Diocese during his twelve years in office. The Bishop would defend such appointments on the grounds that he could rely most on those he knew really well. Generally speaking Dr. Mortimer made good appointments and built up a happy team spirit among his clergy.

Bishop Clarke remained as Bishop and Archdeacon of Plymouth until his retirement in 1962. In his place the Bishop recommended to the Crown the Ven. W.G. Sanderson, who had come to the Diocese as Rector of Silverton in 1954 and had been appointed Archdeacon of Barnstaple in 1959. This rapid promotion of a country incumbent to Suffragan Bishop was rather unusual but Dr. Mortimer chose him as a very good priest and pastor who was suited to high office. An Oxford graduate, Fr. Sanderson was a tall and slender person; his great interest in pastoral matters, including the healing ministry, remained with him. On his retirement in 1972 after an illness, Dr. Mortimer submitted to the Crown as a successor Canon R.F. Cartwright, Vicar of St. Mary Redcliffe for the previous sixteen years. Dr. Mortimer never forgot his happy days at Redcliffe and was regularly in touch with its Vicar and other friends in the parish. Neither Bishop Sanderson nor Bishop Cartwright held the Archdeaconry of Plymouth; on Bishop Clarke's retirement Dr. Mortimer decided to separate the offices of Bishop and Archdeacon of Plymouth, and from 1962-78 the Ven. F.A.J. Matthews successfully combined two very demanding jobs, the Archdeaconry and the Vicarage of the large parish of Plympton St. Mary.

The other Suffragan see was the Bishopric of Crediton. On Bishop Mortimer's arrival the Rt. Rev. W.F. Surtees held this post, as he had done since 1930. He was a fine Christian who worked extremely happily with Dr. Mortimer, and latterly he was grey-haired and venerable in appearance. 82 years of age in 1953, he seemed as strong and active as ever, but the next year he became suddenly crippled with arthritis and had to retire; two years later he died.

As his successor Dr. Mortimer recommended to the Crown the Ven. Wilfrid A. Westall, Archdeacon of Exeter since 1951. The son of a former Exeter incumbent, Fr. Westall had been a friend of the Bishop's since he had once preached at Keble College Chapel during Dr. Mortimer's undergraduate days. After twelve years as Vicar of a Brighton parish and three years as a Country Missioner in York Diocese, he had come to the Diocese as Vicar of Shaldon in 1945. Dr. Mortimer was delighted to find him in the Diocese on his appointment to Exeter and although Fr. Westall had expected to spend the rest of his days at Shaldon - he was already over 50 - Dr. Mortimer persuaded him to accept the Archdeaconry, which carried a Residentiary Canonry. Bishop Westall remembers saying to him: "I am no committee man and I have always tried to avoid Archdeacons. Why do you want me, of all people, to be one of your bureaucrats?" "Well, we've got to have them, but I just want you to be with me," was Dr. Mortimer's reply. Fr. Westall's remarkably warm, friendly and outgoing personality, his ability to be "all things to all men" and his great gifts as a witty and interesting speaker had already found their mark in the Diocese. "He is too well-known in the Diocese to need any further introduction," wrote Dr. Mortimer when announcing his appointment as Archdeacon, "I am certain that both the Archdeaconry and the Cathedral will from the outset feel the benefit and stimulus of his great personal gifts."

These words certainly came true and when writing of Archdeacon Westall's appointment as Bishop of Crediton Dr. Mortimer added "I know that the Archdeacon has been overwhelmed with congratulatory letters from all over the country." Bishop Westall became one of his Diocesan's closest friends and Dr. Mortimer used to speak of him as "my perfect foil". Bishop Westall was more popular than Dr. Mortimer with the ordinary parishioners because of his warm friendliness and winning ways in the Church Hall after the service and the great wit and humanity in his sermons. But over against this Dr. Mortimer was the wise and able administrator, the theologian whose intellectual acumen kept the Diocese and churchpeople on a sound and creative course, the shy but kindly leader whose pastoral heart helped far more people than was popularly realised. For twenty years the two Bishops worked in double harness and Dr. Mortimer would regularly ask his colleague to take on those pastoral chores which he thought he could not tackle himself.

This was a great tribute to Dr. Mortimer's large-mindedness. Many other men in the same position would have been very chary of appointing as their deputy someone who was likely to be more popular than themselves! But Robert Mortimer never worried about this; knowing that his rather retiring manner was in certain respects a handicap in discharging pastoral duties, he was only too happy to choose as his lieutenant someone who he felt could make up for his own shortcomings. The two Bishops became such close friends that Bishop Westall claimed that he could usually guess what was in Dr. Mortimer's mind and predict in advance how the Diocesan would react to a certain situation: "I was rarely wrong."

As the Deans of the Cathedral were appointed by the Crown, apart from unofficial consultations the Bishop had no voice in choosing them. When he came to Exeter Dr. S.C. Carpenter, a delightful elderly scholar who might have been one of the Caroline divines, had been Dean since 1934. Despite the difference in age the two men at once developed a mutual respect and worked very happily together. Of his Bishop, Dr. Carpenter wrote in 1950: "And now we have Bishop Robert Mortimer, young and eager, a man of devoted will, a pastoral spirit, a keen intellect, 'throughly furnished unto all good works', with special knowledge of Moral Theology and of the Canon and customs of the Church and still a cricketer(!)" The Dean retired in 1950; on his death in 1959 Dr. Mortimer wrote "He was a great scholar, a great Christian and a great gentleman."

Dr. Carpenter's successor was Canon A.R. Wallace who had been Headmaster of Sherborne from 1934-50 and Headmaster of Blundell's School before that. He came almost straight to the Deanery from Sherborne and it was said by some that he did not adequately appreciate the difference between running a Cathedral and running a Public School. However he launched the Cathedral Restoration Appeal in 1951 and successfully saw through substantial restorations, including the replacing of the West Window and the cleaning of the West Front. He retired in 1960.

Dean Wallace's successor was Canon Marcus Knight, who had been a priest-vicar of Exeter Cathedral in the 'thirties and then Vicar of Cockington, Torquay from 1937-40 before serving as a Canon Residentiary of St. Paul's Cathedral from 1944-60. Dean Knight launched another Cathedral Appeal in 1965 and the very extensive restoration which followed included the cleaning of the rest of the Cathedral, with its massive towers, giving the Mother Church an unbelievably new appearance, the grey-black stone turning to a soft yellow sandstone hue. On the Dean's retirement in 1972, the Bishop, who had worked very happily with him, wrote: "During his period of office, great things have been done in and for the Cathedral. The standard of worship had steadily improved, the congregation have increased and a happy family relationship in the congregations has been established. There has also been the successful Cathedral Campaign... All this has been, in large part, due to the Dean's leadership."

In 1973 Dr. C.T. Chapman, then Canon Residentiary of Guildford Cathedral, was appointed Dean. He quickly settled down happily, but within months the Bishop had retired.

With four archdeaconries in the Diocese space does not allow a mention of all the Archdeacons who served over the 24 years. Most of them, in fact all of them at the time of the Bishop's retirement, had given good service as parish priests in the Diocese, and all seemed to work happily with the Bishop.

As close to Dr. Mortimer as anyone outside the family was his Domestic Chaplain, Canon F.G. Rice, to whom reference has already been made. Canon Rice, who was born in Exeter and possessed an encyclopaedic knowledge of all the clergy in the Diocese going back at least to the 'thirties, was accepted for ordination by Bishop Cecil and ordained by Dr. Curzon in 1941. Returning to Exeter as Vicar of St. David's in 1953, after a spell in a Plymouth incumbency, he became Honorary Chaplain to the Bishop in 1956. Canon Rice's warm and sympathetic personality soon penetrated the Bishop's retiring manner and the two became very firm friends. Frequently Canon Rice acted as the Bishop's "chauffeur" (though the Bishop's regular chauffeur, Mr. A.J. Chandler, served him well for many years and was remembered in Dr. Mortimer's Will) when he travelled to Confirmations and similar events. The two men developed a great appreciation for each other's sense of humour and Canon Rice became confidant to the Bishop as few others ever became. In 1970 the Bishop appointed him to a Residentiary Canonry at the Cathedral, and after Dr. Mortimer's death the family presented him with the Bishop's pectoral cross in rememberance of the help that he had given.

We now turn to some of the specialist departments of the Diocese. The Bishop's work in the fields of Ordination Training and Education has been covered in other chapters, so it is appropriate to commence with the field of Mission, both in the Diocese and beyond. When Dr. Mortimer came to the Diocese the Diocesan Missioner was Prebendary W.A.P. Dawson, a very able and energetic priest (he was also Director of Ordination Training) who had a great gift for friendship and was noted for the splendid teaching missions which he conducted, particularly in the villages. In 1955 however he had to give up the work of Diocesan Missioner because of illness and in 1957 he died suddenly at only 44 years of age. In his place the Bishop appointed the Rev. H.E. Kendall, the former Warden of St. Edward's School, who had come to Exeter as Rector of St. Mary Arches. This was perhaps not the most successful of Dr. Mortimer's appointments, since Fr. Kendall seemed to be rather tired out after his many years at St. Edward's, and few developments took place during his time in the Diocese. He resigned in 1961 and died in 1963.

In 1964 the Bishop appointed the Rev. G.A. Willis as Diocesan Missioner. Prebendary Willis, as he later became, had qualified as a veterinary surgeon before training for the ministry at Ely Theological College under Canon Balmforth, and had previously been Vicar of St. Stephen's, Cheltenham. He was also Rector of St. Martin's, St. Stephen's and St. Lawrence's Churches in central Exeter at this time.

The Bishop saw mission as part of the continuing life of the local church and he felt that the main task was to help train the laity to play their part of service and witness in their daily lives. In this connection Prebendary Willis arranged many laity-training conferences, both in residential centres and in the parishes. The Bishop did not seem to favour the large Parochial Mission, but he was anxious that nationally organised efforts, such as the "No Small Change" Campaign of 1964, should penetrate to all the parishes. In this campaign, which was designed to arouse the laity to deeper commitment and stewardship, he commissioned sixty laymen, who were trained by Prebendary Willis and others, as "Bishop's Envoys" to visit the parishes. When "The People Next Door" campaign came a few years later the Bishop gave his support to a large number of ecumenical house groups. This was probably the first time that Christians of all denominations had looked together at their responsibilities on such a large scale in the Diocese. Dr. Mortimer seconded the Vicar of Broadclyst, the Rev. David Wardrop, to be national organiser of this campaign, and released him from his parish for several months.

The Bishop was equally keen on Overseas Mission work. When the MRI (Mutual Responsibility and Interdependence in the Body of Christ) campaign was launched in 1964 after the Toronto Conference, although he strongly criticised the title, he was most anxious for the Diocese to make a proper response. As a result £3,000 a year from the Parochial Share or 'Quota' was voted to the Diocese of Rangoon, and the Bishop of Rangoon was invited to preach in Exeter Cathedral. Some layfolk, and perhaps clergy too, felt that donations to Missions should not be "extracted" via the Quota, but the system went on until the Bishop retired, and at least it was a somewhat unique effort in support of the Church Overseas. It may be added that Exeter Diocese, though far from being either the most affluent or populous, was very generous in its missionary giving at this time. In 1966 £49,000 was given by the Diocese, which amounted to no less than 5p a head from every man, woman and child in Devon.

Another vital area of concern was the Moral Welfare Council, or as it later became, the Diocesan Council for Family and Social Welfare. Dr. Mortimer took great interest in this; not only was he President, but he frequently took the chair at its quarterly Executive meetings. Under his guidance the Council greatly prospered. When he came the staff consisted of an Organising Secretary, and one social worker, but by the time he retired there were an Organising Secretary, six "Josephine Butler" trained social workers with their part-time typists, an Adoption Society with its Adoption Secretary and the St. Nicholas Mother and Baby Home at Alphington.

Both these latter institutions were inspired by the Bishop himself. He used his influence in co-operation with Mr. K. Brill (Children's Officer of Devon County Council) and Mrs. E.F. Glenn (Secretary and Treasurer of the

Diocesan Council) to set up the grant-aided Diocesan Adoption Committee, which became the largest Voluntary Adoption Society in the South-West. In 1972 seventy-six babies were placed in homes. As regards the Mother and Baby Home, the Bishop was so much involved in its setting-up that all concerned wanted to call it Mortimer House, but the Bishop was sternly against the idea! Owing to a sharply decreasing need for such homes, the St. Nicholas Home was closed in 1974, but for twenty years (for sixteen of which Miss M. Leyman was Matron) it did a fine job, caring in its hey-day for over 50 girls each year. A second such home at Lympstone, called Exmouth House, was opened in 1962, but it had to be closed in 1968 because of disciplinary troubles - as the Annual Report stated at the closure, of the 34 girls who had passed through the Home six were happily married, three of them to Royal Marines!

When the Organising Secretary, Miss M.K. Leslie, retired in 1968, the Tavistock Deanery forwarded to the Bishop a resolution that her successor should be an 'ecumenical appointment'. Taking up the suggestion at once, Dr. Mortimer contacted the Rev. W.T. Cowlan, a Baptist Minister from Bournemouth who for the last five years had been Vice-Chairman of the Somerset Churches' Moral Welfare Association. Mr. Cowlan agreed to become Organising Secretary provided that the Baptist Union were ready to second him to this work, as indeed they were. The arrangement worked most happily and greatly increased co-operation between the denominations over social problems. Even before Mr. Cowlan's appointment some of the four or five Archdeaconry Services of Offering, to which the parishes brought their annual gift towards the Council's work, were held in Free Churches, or with Free Church preachers. Over recent years the Free Churches have given this work considerable support - it must surely be the care of all Christians.

Another notable event took place in 1972 when the Council for Family and Social Welfare moved from its old offices in the Palace Gatehouse to spacious new premises at Glenn House, 96 Old Tiverton Road, which the Diocesan Board of Finance provided; the Bishop himself performed the opening ceremony. In that year the Diocese's social workers helped no less than 484 clients; 392 of these concerned illegitimacy and 92 had marital, social or moral problems. Dr. Mortimer also presided at the meeting at the City Library, the chief speaker being Miss (now Dame) G. Aves, out of which the Voluntary Workers' Bureau at Exeter sprang up, the first of its kind in Devon. Similar Bureaux sprang up in Torbay, Plymouth, Newton Abbot, Tavistock and Barnstaple.

A particularly important part of Diocesan activity is the Diocesan Office which is headquarters of the Board of Finance. For most of the Bishop's reign this was situate in the administrative wing of the Palace, with the Bishop's Office just around the corner. When Dr. Mortimer came to Exeter the Secretary of the Diocesan Board of Finance was Prebendary W. Gabriel Harris. He had been very successful, but just as Prebendary Dawson did later on he worked so hard at the job that his health was undermined and he had to retire in 1951. The Bishop approved the appointment of Mr. E.J.N. Wallis, C.B.E. as his successor. Mr. Wallis discharged the duties very well for eight years before moving to the post of Christian Stewardship Adviser for the Diocese. His place was taken by Miss K.J. Le Clair, M.B.E., who had already been at the Diocesan Office for over ten years and continued as Diocesan Secretary for another eighteen years before she retired in 1977.

Miss Le Clair's serene manner coupled with her marked administrative ability enabled her to discharge the work with distinction over this long spell. She worked most happily with the Bishop, of whom she wrote: "The complete faith in those to whom he delegated some of his administrative duties, resulted in his winning the complete loyalty and deep affection of those to whom he had delegated. One just could not betray such absolute trust. A few minutes in his office was like an oasis of peace in a day of chaos and turmoil. The calm of his bearing and the peace of his eyes soon dispersed the tensions which had built up during the day. His care and concern for even the most junior member of the staff was always evident.... One knew instinctively, and gained courage from the knowledge, that one's cares were remembered in his prayers."

As an expert amateur journalist in his younger days, the Bishop was naturally interested in this side of affairs. Dr. Curzon had founded the *Exeter Diocesan Leaflet*, which under the able care of Prebendary Harris had risen to a circulation of over 50,000, mainly as a parish magazine inset. Like Dr. Curzon, Dr. Mortimer edited the four-page leaflet himself, and with the help of first Prebendary Harris and then Mr. Wallis as Honorary Secretary it rose to a peak circulation of over 71,000 copies a month in 1965. Usually over a third of the space was given to the Bishop's article; the exceptionally fine quality of these articles, which rivalled those of Archbishop Garbett in the *York Diocesan Leaflet*, has been alluded to elsewhere. The format of the leaflet, however, was very unexciting. Until 1968 the Bishop simply continued in Dr. Curzon's style, with dull off-white paper and an absolute minimum of attractive type or display. In 1968 the *Leaflet* was given a "face lift" at no extra cost to the parishes - from henceforth it was printed on fine white paper with rather nicer type. Even so a film-strip created by an Evangelical organisation portrayed the front page of one issue of the new-style *Leaflet*, with an article by the Bishop on Moral Theology, as an example of how not to preach the Gospel!

However, the operative phrase here is "at no extra cost to the parishes." Parish Magazines have to sell at a sufficiently low price to attract as many purchasers as possible, and most contain some inset, besides the *Diocesan Leaflet* and the parish's own news. The inflationary post-war period necessitated that costs be kept to an absolute minimum, so that there had to be a very economical format. Furthermore, as the *Leaflet* was of only four pages it was essential to cram the maximum amount of information into this restricted space. Many other dioceses had Leaflets of similar style.

Again, if the *Diocesan Leaflet* was a trifle ordinary in style, this could certainly not be said of the exciting new Diocesan newspaper *Venture*, which made its bow in January 1963. This owed much to its brilliant first Editor,

Dr. H.B. Graham, who had moved from a northern diocese to Devon as Vicar of Blackawton. But it was launched with Dr. Mortimer's full support and encouragement - with his immensely busy life the Bishop could not possibly have taken on the editorial pen himself. Of the size and style of a tabloid newspaper and graced by fine photographs and a most attractive lay-out, *Venture* had a popular appeal which very few other diocesan journals could match. One of its chief virtues was that it appealed to the ordinary churchgoer - it gave month-by-month news of what people were doing in the parishes - rather than adopting that quasi-intellectual style beloved of most Church newspapers.

Although *Venture*, initially priced at 4d, was an instant success, it did later have difficulties over its circulation, which never approached the 20,000 copies hoped for. This was for the simple reason that almost all churchgoers bought a parish magazine each month, and to buy *Venture* as well was more than they were prepared to do. A scheme for parishes to sell *Venture*, with inset pages of parish news, **instead** of the parish magazine, never caught on to the extent that was hoped. The first crisis came only seven months after the paper had been launched, with the tragic death of Dr. Graham in August 1963. However, the Rev. F.W.T. Fuller, Chaplain of St. Luke's College, agreed to take on the Editorship and *Venture* continued to go ahead. It was in June 1969, after the circulation had fallen somewhat to 8,000, that the Bishop sadly announced that the paper would have to be temporarily discontinued for financial reasons. But thanks to a handsome donation which was sufficient to meet any possible losses for three years, *New Venture* commenced in June 1970, under the editorship of Prebendary J.F. Parkinson, the Bishop's Public Relations Officer. It was much in the same style as the old *Venture*, and to the great credit of all concerned it continues to this day.

During Dr. Mortimer's episcopate a number of new churches were built. In October 1956 no less than four were consecrated by the Bishop: St. Francis', Honicknowle; St. Chad's, Whitleigh and St. Peter's, all in Plymouth, and the new St. James', Exeter. Two months later the nearly rebuilt St. Marychurch, and the enlarged Shiphay Church, both in Torquay, were consecrated. St. Luke's, Milber was consecrated in 1955 and St. Andrew's, Tiverton, built to serve a new housing area, in 1971. Despite his keenness to build new churches in areas of growing population, however, the Bishop was wedded to the old and historic as far as church buildings were concerned. He was very sad when old and large vicarages had to be sold. He accepted the need for smaller houses but thought it a retrograde step!

The Bishop was much interested in the Diocesan Registrar's work. As a Canonist he was an expert on Church law, but his interest extended to all laws, especially those concerned with marriage, divorce and other human situations. When Sir Godwin Michelmore received the K.B.E. in 1953 the Bishop wrote: "I doubt if any other Diocese has a K.B.E. for its Registrar. But Exeter has known for long that it has been peculiarly fortunate, and we all rejoice that Sir Godwin's public services have been thus publicly recognised." In 1963 after an illness Sir Godwin resigned and the Bishop appointed his son, Mr. J.F.G. Michelmore, in his place. Sir Godwin assisted thereafter as Deputy Registrar; years before his own father had changed places with him in the same way. From an outsider's viewpoint it seemed that the legal affairs of the Diocese were in extremely capable hands with Mr. W.S. Wigglesworth, one of the Church of England's most celebrated lawyers, as Chancellor (later to be succeeded by Mr. David Calcutt, Q.C.) and the Michelmore family providing the Registrar.

The bishop's enthusiasm for sport was not without its repercussions in Diocesan affairs! The Clergy Golfing Society, although previously approved by Bishop Curzon, did not actually commence until November 1949 when it was started personally by Dr. Mortimer with the Rev. Gordon Samuel as Secretary. Some twenty clergy joined; they met about once a month, usually on a Monday, on various golf courses all over Devon, having lunch together during the proceedings. The Bishop himself was not a great golfer but he enjoyed these sessions immensely. He particularly liked to play with his friend the Rev. Henry

Kendall - the story that these two overcame the hazards of bunkers by kicking the ball out sideways was widespread but this one probably was aprocryphal!

The golfing highlight of the year for the Bishop was playing for the De La Rue Cup. At the time Bishop Westall's brother was Managing Director of De La Rue; he used to bring a team of four and stay either at the Manor House Hotel, Moretonhampstead or the Saunton Sands Hotel near the Saunton course. The Bishop and his team stayed at the same hotel as Mr. Westall's guests and the two fours competed for the cup. Fortunes varied over the years but the Bishop's team won the last three. Prebendary Samuel was succeeded as Secretary by Prebendary E.P. James, M.B.E., who kindly sent most of this information.

The second official sporting activity in the Diocese was the Clergy Cricket Club which was formed, with thirty members, late in 1951. The Secretary was the Rev. C.G. Dawe, and in the opening season at least one match was played each week. The Bishop gave his full support, and sometimes played himself. The Club had its ups and downs; often there was a shortage of players and in 1964 the entire summer programme had to be cancelled for this reason. In that year in the *Exeter Diocesan Leaflet* the Bishop wrote: "My opinion is that it would do nothing but good if the clergy, and especially the curates, take a second day off a week to meet some of the laity on the cricket fields or the golf links. Will Vicars kindly note and Curates remind them!" However the Club's year of triumph came in 1971 when they were runners-up in the *Church Times* Cricket Cup, with thirty one dioceses competing.

CHAPTER XI

Notable Events while Bishop of Exeter

In this chapter we recount various events which were milestones in the Bishop's life but which do not fit into the pattern of the other chapters. The first came in July 1950 when the 900th Anniversary of the founding of the Diocese was celebrated. The original see had been at Crediton ("When Exeter was a fuzzy down, Crediton was a market town"), which had had a Bishop at least since 909. But in 1050 Leofric, who had held the sees of Crediton and Cornwall since 1046, moved the see to the walled city of Exeter to protect it from despoiliation by the Danes and the Irish. In that year he had the honour of being enthroned as the first Bishop of Exeter by King Edward the Confessor in the small Saxon church on the present Cathedral site.

At a great Evensong in the Cathedral on Monday July 10th at 4.15 p.m. the King and Queen walked together in the procession with Princess Margaret behind them. They followed the Bishop of Exeter and the Bishop of Crediton and were greeted on their entrance by a fanfare from the State Trumpeters of the Household Cavalry. A vast congregation including the Bishop of Truro and other bishops, the clergy of the Diocese and civic dignitaries representing both City and County, packed the Cathedral. Afterwards the Royal Family drove through the heavily bomb-damaged streets and saw plans for rebuilding the city centre.

On July 20th at 6.30 p.m. a service was held at Crediton Church to mark the transference of the see. Dr. Mortimer and his Suffragans attended and on their return they were greeted by the Mayor and Corporation at Eastgate and proceeded to the Cathedral for a short service of thanksgiving. On July 21st Dr. Curzon, the previous Bishop of Exeter, preached at Choral Eucharist at the Cathedral at 11.30 a.m. and at 3 p.m. the celebrations concluded with another great service at which the Archbishop of Canterbury, Dr. Fisher, was the preacher. The services were relayed to the Cathedral Green for those unable to find a place in the Cathedral and on July 21st lunch and tea were available in the Palace grounds.

In May 1951 the Bishop visited the U.S.A. and on his return addressed the Diocesan Conference on the Protestant Episcopal Church, the Anglican Church of that land. Two things about it won Dr. Mortimer's admiration. First, it was much more consciously a missionary church than was the Church of England, and secondly the generosity of the American laity was superb: "I was astounded at the magnitude of the contributions made by ordinary churchmen."

The Bishop did not admire the procedure for selecting ordinands in the U.S.A., however, which seemed to him to infringe the ancient rights of a bishop! In the States a Bishop could not ordain anyone without the consent of his Standing Committee, half of whom were laymen. "It seems to me that the American genius for organisation has overreached itself," he commented, and said he much preferred the English C.A.C.T.M. Selection Boards! Dr. Mortimer was surprised, too, at the little power the American bishop had in appointing priests to benefices. The Vestry made the election, the Bishop merely had to be satisfied that the candidate was a 'duly qualified minister'. "There appears to be no Institution, and the role of the Bishop, as chief Pastor and responsible for the filling of every cure, is gravely under-estimated," he added.

1953 was Coronation year. The Bishop was delighted to attend the historic service in Westminster Abbey and amongst his personal treasures was the letter commanding attendance, personally signed by the Queen and the Duke of Norfolk. He issued special forms of service to be used throughout the Diocese on Trinity Sunday, May 31st, and encouraged the participation of other denominations. The Queen had graciously agreed that the collections at Anglican services that day be given to the Ordination Candidates' Fund.

Soon after, on June 29th, commenced a Week of Thanksgiving for the Restoration of the Cathedral after war damage, which was now completed. At the Solemn Eucharist on that day the Bishop consecrated St. Andrew's and St. James' Chapels in the Cathedral, both restored after serious damage. In the afternoon, Dr. W.R. Matthews, the distinguished Dean of St. Paul's who had been Dean of Exeter from 1931-34, was the preacher at Evensong. 1953 was also the 400th Anniversary of the birth in Exeter of Richard Hooker, the great Anglican divine. The Bishop arranged for Mr. C.S. Lewis to lecture on Hooker at the Annual Clergy School in July, the lectures on this occasion being open to the public.

The same year we were on the threshold of Sponsored Television and the Bishop surprised some of his followers by confessing: "I have got no T.V. in my own house. I do not know, at first hand, what is the effect of T.V. on family life. But it is obvious to anyone that the effect must be enormous for good or ill." Although the Government were going to set up a national council to safeguard the quality of programmes, the Bishop's fears were not allayed. His advice was "Let's not risk it;" he was going to ask his M.P. to vote against it. In retrospect the Bishop's anxiety seems hard to understand, for even if ITV to-day is far from perfect, B.B.C. programmes do not seem all that superior! But no one at the time had any idea what the ITV programmes would be like and many thought that the advertising element in the broadcasts would be far more aggresive than in fact it was.

Next came the 1200th Anniversary of the death of St. Boniface, the great missionary who was born at Crediton, founded a famous abbey at Fulda and played a large part in the conversion of Germany to Christianity before being martyred at Dokkum in present-day Holland. Some took the date of his martyrdom as 754 and others as 755. The Continental celebrations were held in 1954, and the Archbishop of Canterbury asked Dr. Mortimer to represent the Church of England. He preached on St. Boniface at Dokkum on July 3rd and later at Utrecht.

The Exeter Diocesan celebrations were held in 1955. On Saturday June 4th the celebrated Dr. Bell, Bishop of Chichester, preached at Evensong in the Cathedral, and a Pilgrimage from the Cathedral to Crediton Church took place. The next day the televised Ordination already mentioned was held in the Cathedral. The Abbot of Nashdom, an Anglican Benedictine, was asked to preach as

St. Boniface himself was a Benedictine. On June 7th the Archbishop of Canterbury preached at Festal Evensong at the Cathedral, two laymen from every parish being invited as well as the clergy.

Two months earlier, from April 19th-21st, the Bishop had held in the Cathedral a Synod for all the Diocesan clergy entitled "The Life and Duties of the Clergy". He gave a very searching Charge to his clergy, covering almost every aspect of the priest's life, which was later published as a pamphlet. But the main purpose of the Synod, as Dr. Mortimer freely admitted, was for him to learn how the ministry in the parishes was working out in the rapidly changing situation. The following year he held an Episcopal Visitation throughout the Diocese.

In November 1956 the Bishop was much in the news over his public statement in support of Sir Anthony Eden on his intervention in the Suez crisis. In July 1956 Colonel Nasser had announced, after the U.S.A. had withdrawn the offer of a loan to help Egypt build the Aswan Dam, that the Suez Canal Company was to be unilaterally "nationalised" by Egypt. On July 30th Sir Anthony declared that Britain could not agree to Egypt's unfettered control of the Canal and that certain reservists would be called up in case military action became necessary. When all attempts to find a peaceful settlement had failed and Israel had invaded the Sinai Peninsula on October 28th, Eden, without previously consulting the United Nations, the Commonwealth or the U.S.A., announced in the House of Commons that the British and French Governments had sent an ultimatum to Nasser warning him that their forces would occupy the Canal area if hostilities did not cease.

When on November 5th the threatened invasion of Suez took place, Eden found himself the most unpopular man on earth! The old days, when Britain had sufficient prestige and power to intervene in what seemed a just cause, had passed away. All the do-gooders censured Eden as a warmonger, or at very least for disregarding the authority of the United Nations. But not so Dr. Mortimer! Addressing the Diocesan Conference on November 6th he said; "I am bound to admire a man who has the courage of his convictions and to dissociate myself emphatically from any attack on his personal honour." Allowing that Sir Anthony's judgement **might** have been wrong, the Bishop left his hearers in no doubt that he thought it was right. Peace was not maintained, he said, simply by saying 'Let there be peace, do not fight'. If Eden had struck a blow at the United Nations, he believed it was the blow of the surgeon's knife, not of the assassin's cudgel.

In about a month, under heavy pressure from the U.S.A., the Prime Minister was forced to withdraw the troops from Suez. By January 1957 he had resigned on medical advice and his political career was virtually at an end. Dr. Mortimer may have been one of a tiny minority supporting Eden, and the verdict of historians so far seems to be that Sir Anthony made a serious miscalculation in deciding to invade Suez. Be that as it may, the Bishop's courage and sincerity in defending Sir Anthony in the face of almost universal popular condemnation cannot but be admired.

From July 3rd - August 10th 1958 the Bishop attended the first of his two Lambeth Conferences. As usual some of the Overseas Bishops toured the dioceses beforehand; four of them visited various parishes in Exeter Diocese. They were warmly welcomed by the Bishop and all attended the Sung Eucharist at the Cathedral on June 18th, Bishop Robin (formerly of Adelaide) being the preacher. The Conference came at a very significant time, when the post-war desire for reform and development was at its height. Great questions such as Bible Interpretation, Prayer Book Revision, the Reunion Schemes for North India and Ceylon, Peace and War in the Nuclear Age, and the Place of the Family in Modern Society were discussed.

Dr. Mortimer was greatly impressed by the spirit of unity and fellowship at the Conference. There were differences of opinion, sometimes sharp differences, he wrote - but in nearly every case a considerable measure of agreement was reached after discussion. Many Bishops who had also attended the 1948 Conference commented on the greater friendliness and understanding shown at this one. The Bishop was especially interested at the contributions from the new nations. Asian Bishops pointed out that if European Bishops used military metaphors such as "missionary strategy", this could easily be twisted to imply concepts of Western Imperialism! South African Bishops stressed how much moral courage was needed to support a more liberal policy towards the colour-bar, while other African Bishops explained the acute difficulties of preaching monogamy in countries where polygamy was freely allowed. Many non-white Bishops stressed the all-pervading influence of racialism and nationalism in their lands, such that Christianity would be severely handicapped until national churches with a native ministry and native rites could emerge. Dr. Mortimer came away with a deep and lasting impression of the Anglican Communion as a close-knit family of autonomous churches.

In 1960 the Bishop's sermon in Upton Parish Church on June 19th, addressed to members of the British Medical Association who were gathered at Torquay for their Annual Meetings, caused quite a stir in the national press - even *The Times* devoted a lesser leader to the subject. The Bishop said that while ordinary means should be employed to keep very old people alive, there was no obligation to use extraordinary means, which he defined as means involving very great expense, inconvenience or hardship and which at the same time offered no reasonable expectation of success or benefit to the patient. "To subject very old people to the acute discomfort of a serious operation, or of feeding by intravenous drip would seem to be morally wrong. Such means should only be used when there was reasonable hope of recovery or where some benefit or happiness was conferred on the patient. In other words, in this field of medicine there seems to be some truth in the old couplet 'Thou shalt not kill, but needest not strive officiously to keep alive'."

Few Bishops have the expertise to address doctors in this manner, of course, and Dr. Mortimer's teaching was in full accord with the best traditions of Moral Theology. His point was that doctors, keen as they were to save life in accordance with the high ideals of their profession, sometimes went a little too far in putting very elderly people, who had naturally reached the end of their time, through painful operations which at best added a few months to their life and might be a complete failure. As

The Times interpreted it, though, the Bishop had raised the issue 'Is an old person's life less valuable than anyone else's?' which was in fact far from his mind.

The paper felt that the majority of doctors would probably agree with the Bishop, "yet many misgivings are bound to be aroused . . . . How would 'extraordinary means' be defined? The Bishop's definition virtually begs the question, for he does not define 'very great expense' &c. Ideally anyone, young or old, whose life could be saved by an operation should be able to undergo it."

Few thinking Christians would disagree with Dr. Mortimer on this point, though there can be no inflexible rule. Every patient is a person in his own right and the correct decision can only be made if the fullest care is given to his individual circumstances.

In the same address the Bishop made a very shrewd point, so often unnoticed by those who love to argue on such matters, "I do not myself believe that in this country euthanasia is a live issue at all. It is rather a matter of academic discussion and in this respect it is very important to distinguish clearly between euthanasia and the administration of pain-relieving drugs in lethal quantities." The Bishop added that it was the doctor's duty, besides saving life, to use every possible means to alleviate pain. In some cases he had to give drugs in such large doses to relieve pain that he shortened the life of his patient and finally ended it. He had not failed in his duty in doing so, nor had he been disloyal to his oath to save life.

In September 1960 Dr. Mortimer made one of his numerous visits to the U.S.A., for some weeks on a lecture tour. This time, however, he undertook a Teaching Crusade at St. Matthew's, Wheeling in West Virginia Diocese. Afterwards he preached the Hale Memorial Sermon at Seabury-Western Theological Seminary, Evanston, one of the leading theological colleges in the States. His subject was "The Nature and Purpose of Canon Law". He spent two or three weeks in West Virginia Diocese, which led to an interesting exchange. In October 1961 the Bishop of West Virginia, thirty of his clergy and fifteen clergy wives, spent eleven days in Exeter Diocese, paying their own fares and staying at Vicarages and at the homes of laymen. Then in April 1964 a similar party from Exeter Diocese, including Dr. Mortimer, spent over three weeks in West Virginia. Both sides not only enjoyed the exchange but learned a great deal about each other's Churches, both Anglican, yet so different in the details of their working. In between these trips, from January 10th-31st 1963, Dr. Mortimer attended and presented a paper at the Conference in Chicago on Radiation and Social Ethics. Only seven months later, in August 1963, the Bishop and his Suffragans were in Canada for ten days, attending the Worldwide Anglican Conference at Toronto which produced the famous document on MRI.

In no time, as it seemed, the Bishop's second Lambeth Conference had come around. The Bishops gathered at Church House, Westminster in August 1968 and this time suffragan bishops took part, so the Bishops of Exeter, Crediton and Plymouth were all there. Dr. Mortimer's enthusiasm for the Conference was noticeably less than in 1958, however, doubtless because, being already 65 years of age and with responsibilities as heavy as ever, he was feeling the weight of his advancing years. As in 1958 several Overseas Bishops preached in the parishes of the Diocese on August 4th and 11th. The Bishop wrote no full-length article on Lambeth in the *Diocesan Leaflet,* but in a brief note in the October issue he commented: "I found the Conference an exhausting business. Listening to speeches all day long for several days is tedious. I made, I think, four speeches myself - which must surely be three too many. All the same, the Conference was well worth while and in the reports of the three Sections there is much good stuff." He suggested that the Conference Report would make good Advent study material.

In one of his four speeches Dr. Mortimer opposed resolutions favouring joint participation in the Eucharist by Anglicans and non-episcopal Churches. In the current Ecumenical atmosphere there was massive support for the resolutions and the Bishop of Lincoln, Dr. Riches, for example, declared that Anglicans were in danger of killing a beauty and a loveliness by continuing vendettas from a past age. Dr. Mortimer countered that it was precisely because the pace of change was so rapid that in the excitement and hurry they might let slip something that was of immense importance. "I want unity, I pray for unity," he said, "but I have been brought to believe that in God's time this unity will come and that it will be based on the Lambeth Quadrilateral."

The year 1969 saw the 600th Anniversary of the death of Bishop John Grandisson who built the glorious Nave of the Cathedral; after his death the building was substantially as it is to-day. A great service was held in the Mother Church on the afternoon of Tuesday July 15th - a lovely summer day. The preacher was the Archbishop of Canterbury; he and Mrs. Ramsey arrived the day before and stayed with the Dean and his wife. The guest of honour was the Queen Mother, who was welcomed by the Bishop and the Dean at the door of the Cathedral and on her entry was greeted by a fanfare of trumpets. The same evening the Archbishop and Mrs. Ramsey saw a *Son et Lumière* performance at the Cathedral - the first they had ever seen.

1970 was the 21st Anniversary of Dr. Mortimer's Consecration. The Bishop said that he felt tired after so many years' service, and it was appropriate that he should have a long holiday. So in January he and Mrs. Mortimer went abroad for three months. Of this six weeks was spent in India, four weeks at sea and, for the Bishop, four weeks in Africa. Mrs. Mortimer did not go to Africa but instead flew home from Bombay en route for the United States, where she visited her two daughters and saw her first grandchild. The Mortimers stayed at Calcutta with the Metropolitan of India, the Most Rev. H.L.J. de Mel, the Bishop's contemporary at Keble, for part of the time. They also saw something of the work of three Anglican Religious Communities who were giving great help to the very poor by running free or nearly free schools and hospitals. Children brought to them in a terrible physical condition were nursed back to health and strength and given a fine schooling which equipped them to earn their living later on.

The Bishop was fascinated by India which, he said, had a charm and a grandeur all of its own. The children there were happy and always laughing. Except where extreme poverty prevented it they were given loving care by their parents and often by older brothers and sisters. But the population explosion was causing an almost insoluble problem - the rate at which new jobs were being created was continually outpaced by the rate at which the population increased. Not surprisingly one saw large posters everywhere advertising the Government's Family Planning Campaign. But the Green Revolution, aimed at improving agricultural methods, had done much to better the position over the last five years. The Bishop did not give his impressions of South Africa - everyone, he felt, was heartily sick of talk about Apartheid and would not want to hear any more!

On April 25th 1970, the exact 21st Anniversary of the Bishop's Consecration, there was a Sung Eucharist in the Cathedral at 11.15 a.m.; the Bishop celebrated, assisted by his two Suffragans. Every priest in the Diocese was invited, and the congregation of over a thousand also included lay people from all the parishes. The Bishop was very moved at the warmth of the reception given to him. 1970 was indeed a notable year; in June Dr. Mortimer and Bishop Westall led a pilgrimage of forty Christians to Fulda for the St. Boniface Festival, proceeding then to Oberammergau for the Passion Play. The Bishop also represented the Archbishop of Canterbury at the Old Catholic Church Centenary celebrations at Bonn.

On November 15th 1970 came the first meeting of the Exeter Diocesan Synod, the smaller, elected body which had replaced the Diocesan Conference. The Bishop was sad at the passing of the Conference, as were many others. As he said, the huge Conference was hopeless as a legislative body and not very good for debates. But it did, in a sense, bring the Diocese together and give it corporate expression. The Conference was, in fact, a valuable occasion on which to meet clergy and laity from all the parishes, whereas only a small fraction of the parishes were represented on the Diocesan Synod.

On November 9th 1972 the Bishop was in Assisi to take part in the formal acceptance by the Bishop of Fulham and Gibraltar of the Church of S. Gregorio, which the Roman Catholic authorities were lending for the use of non-Roman Catholic pilgrims. Dr. Mortimer gave the official address of thanks from the Anglican Communion on the Archbishop's behalf. He pointed out that the life and devotion of St. Francis had captured the imagination of a great many non-Catholics - the Anglican Franciscans, of whom he was Bishop-Protector, were now the most numerous religious order in the Church of England. The provision of the church was an act of love by the Roman authorities for their "separated brethren", and was accepted with humble gratitude and joy.

A little earlier, in December 1971, the Bishop was in the news because he had given his full support to a booklet, "A Scheme of Education in Personal Relationships", which Exeter's Education Committee had given to all its teachers. The month before a Topsham man had been fined for keeping his two daughters away from their Primary School as a protest against passages in the book which, he claimed, encouraged homosexuality and masturbation. "Relationships with members of the same sex which are homosexual in nature are not necessarily harmful," the booklet stated, "on the contrary they often provide lasting and enriching experiences. It is an error to assume, and irresponsible by default to let young people assume, that such friendships are undesirable or might lead to undesirable practices." The booklet, which made a similar comment on masturbation, was written in the language of what cynics might call do-gooders. While the authors' intentions were certainly good, such language can lead to misunderstanding and there was a considerable "rumpus" when the contents of the booklet became known.

The Bishop pointed out that the booklet was issued to teachers and not to the children. Furthermore, if the booklet were understood in the right way it contained "wise, responsible and pastoral advice and help". Dr. Mortimer was "delighted and astonished" that the Education Committee took it for granted that their teachers "could, should and would exercise enormous pastoral care and concern for the total well-being of the children under their charge." Whether the Bishop was being over-kind in his assessment the reader must judge, but as always he had spoken out with courage.

On January 8th 1973 Dr. Mortimer had the honour of

giving a lecture on Marriage and Divorce at the Gregorian University in Rome. He began by outlining the Church of England's doctrine of marriage, which had changed little at the Reformation. Then in brilliantly lucid style he summarised all the recent legislation in England in this field, from the 1857 Act (by which Register Office marriages were recognised and the right to remarry after divorce allowed in the State law) to the 1969 Divorce Reform Bill in which he himself had played so important a part.

Less than three weeks after this lecture the Bishop saddened the Diocese by announcing his forthcoming retirement. The story of this we must leave to another chapter.

CHAPTER XII

The Bishop on Convocation and Church Assembly

One of Dr. Mortimer's greatest contributions to the life of the Church of England was his work on Canterbury Convocation. His membership of this body spanned almost thirty years, since he had already served in the Lower House for over five years when he was appointed Bishop of Exeter.

In 1944, following Dr. N.P. Williams' death, Dr. Mortimer was elected as one of the two Proctors in Convocation for Oxford University. He was officially welcomed to the Lower House on January 19th 1944 and his maiden speech came in that very first session. The proposed United Church of South India was being discussed and he remarked that the Archbishop should soon state officially whether he encouraged priests from Canterbury Province to join the South Indian Church or not. He added that a statement on the position of Anglican Missionary Societies working in South India was very much needed.

Like all Dr. Mortimer's utterances in Parliament and Convocation, this speech was strictly to the point. The Bishop never spoke on such bodies just for the sake of speaking; he only made a speech if it concerned a matter of real importance on which he had expert knowledge.

The future Bishop introduced himself to Convocation gradually; he made his first major speech in October 1946, by which time he was still not on any of the Convocation's committees. In this speech he opposed an amendment by Preb. P.C. Barber which sought to water down Canon Lindsay Dewar's motion condemning the use of atomic energy to bomb Hiroshima and Nagasaki and deploring the terrible precedent set by these actions. Such a motion seemed to some to be tactless and even undesirable when this bombing had greatly shortened the war against the Japs.

However, Canon Mortimer showed no deference at all to popular patriotic sentiments, for he felt they were completely overruled by the inhumanity of this terrible weapon. The House might not know all the circumstances

with absolute certainty, he said, but they knew enough to
say that the use of atomic bombs on this occasion was not
right. Not for a moment did he pass any moral judgement
on the agents, but he could now see clearly that the action
was wrong. Dr. Mortimer won the day and Canon Dewar's
original motion was carried. As always he had shown the
courage to speak out boldly for what he believed to be
right. As a relative beginner on Convocation he might
have been tempted to use a more conciliatory approach,
for the House was considerably divided on the matter.
Once he was convinced that it was right to do so, however,
he invariably spoke out with neither fear nor favour.

On May 21st 1947 the Report of the Canon Law
Commission came before the Full Synod of Convocation,
and it was Dr. Mortimer's duty to second its formal
acceptance. The Dean of Winchester, who was the
proposer, said in his speech: "I am going to be followed by
one who knows far more about them (the Draft Canons) and
about Canon Law in general than I do, namely Canon
Mortimer." Dr. Mortimer in a learned speech stressed how
much a revised body of Canons was to be desired. If it was
decided to go ahead a preparatory and sifting committee
would be needed. The momentous decision to go ahead was
taken and an extra session of Convocation was arranged for
January 1948 to commence the work. Canon Mortimer now
became a member of the Canon Law Steering Committee
which was to do so much of the preparatory work; the
Canon Law Commission's Draft Canons were taken as the
general basis for the revision.

The next year Mortimer was nominated Bishop of
Exeter, which meant his removal to the Upper House of
Convocation. It was in the Upper House, in fact, where the
Bishop was to play such an illustrious part. The
atmosphere there was relaxed and informal, as between
friends. With only twenty nine bishops at the most
attending, one could make speeches without feeling, as one
did in Full Synod or in the Church Assembly, that there
were thirty others waiting to get a word in! Nor was there
need for the Bishops to couch their speeches in the
language of the layman.

The former Bishop of Leicester, Dr. R.R. Williams,

who kindly gave us his impressions, remembers Robert Mortimer as one of a small group of Bishops, including Dr. Bell of Chichester, Dr. Hunter of Sheffield and Dr. Rawlinson of Derby, who made particularly weighty utterances. Although there were plenty of College Principals and schoolmasters amongst the Bishops, for a fair part of the time Dr. Mortimer was the only University Professor and his great learning, especially where moral questions were concerned, was of special value to Convocation. The standard of debates in the Upper House, Bishop Williams added, was very much higher than in the Full Synod or the Church Assembly. Archdeacon Hilder, formerly Prolocutor of the Lower House, remembers the Bishop in Full Synod as extremely impressive: "he spoke with magisterial authority and precision." There were a few times, a Church official said, when the Bishop "had not done his homework," particularly towards the end of his episcopate when his physical strength seemed to be failing. But in a great many cases the Bishop in a matter of seconds put his finger on the point that mattered, gave a learned, fair and accurate judgement which often carried the House with him.

The Bishop's greatest work on Convocation was without doubt his part in the revision of the Canon Law. As a member of the Archbishops' Commission he had helped to frame the draft Canons which were the basis of the whole revision. Much of the Commission's preliminary work was done on sub-committees, one of which used to meet at Oxford. Dean Addleshaw, who was Honorary Secretary of the Commission and attended these Oxford meetings, relates that Dr. Mortimer's approach was sensible and lively. He wanted to get on with the job, tedious as it seemed to some, and his enthusiasm for the work played a major part in seeing it through to completion. He also showed great wisdom and always seemed to know what should **not** be said! He did not at this stage compose many new clauses for the draft canons.

The Bishop's main work on Canon Law Revision was done in Convocation itself, where the proposed new Canons were all discussed three times over, with a long delay between the second and third readings. The delay was largely caused through Dr. Fisher's sensible desire to refer each canon to the House of Laity before it received final approval. The hold-up was not due to deliberate obstruction on the part of the laity; rather it was because the House of Laity had to debate the Canons by themselves, in such spare moments as they could find, without adequate knowledge of the debates which had taken place in Convocation. It was the resultant frustration - it took over twenty years before the new Canons became law! - that provided the main impetus towards Synodical Government in the Church, in which the laity are brought right into the heart of the governing process.

Our own impression, from a study of the *Chronicle of Canterbury Convocation* over those years, is that Dr. Mortimer's role in these discussions was first that of a wise guide, who knew what would and what would not be acceptable to the widely differing schools of thought in the Church, and secondly as a veritable mine of information and learning. Not only was his wide knowledge of Canon Law unrivalled, but in the absence of learned judges and counsel who were laymen, Dr. Mortimer was generally the person to put Convocation - not to mention the Archbishop! - right on matters of English Statute Law. Any canon which contradicted the law of the land was, of course, automatically void and various cases arose where the wording of a proposed canon was in danger of doing this.

The Bishop also had the lawyer's knack of spotting loopholes in proposed new laws, and phrases not written in the correct legal language. On February 18th 1960, when Dr. Mortimer had proposed that the new Canon 12 be approved by the Full Synod for the first time round, the Bishop of Chester, Dr. Ellison, in supporting him commented that the Bishop of Exeter had spoken with the clarity and brilliance which they always expected of him and never failed to receive. The Provost of Bradford, an Evangelical, speaking just afterwards, added that Dr. Mortimer was one of the most weighty members of the original Canon Law Commission in learning and advice.

We quote a very untypical example to show how the

Bishop's delight in humour intruded even into these discussions. Draft Canon 82 which had been partly taken from the 1603-4 Canon and partly, it is said, composed by Canon Claude Jenkins, ran: "And no Ecclesiastical Person shall wear any Coif or wrought Night-cap, but only plain Night-caps of black silk, satin or velvet!" Dr. Mortimer expressed himself strongly in favour of this wording and when the House accepted the Bishop of Portsmouth's suggestion that it should be amended to "such apparel as shall be suitable to his office," the Bishop of Exeter said that it had been so whittled down that it would be better to omit it altogether!

Dr. Mortimer's other contributions to Convocation, quite apart from Canon Law, would fill a volume of their own and we can only give the barest outline here. The Bishop was particularly interested in Church Union schemes. Whilst with his Catholic background he regarded episcopacy as absolutely essential, he felt the Church's divisions very keenly and especially in his later years he was remarkably tolerant towards Free Church "deviations" from the normal Catholic or Anglican pattern of worship. Bishop R.R. Williams noted that while Dr. Mortimer's earlier contributions to debates were usually strongly weighted on the Catholic side, later on he became affected by the general spirit of unrest and radicalism of the post-war years and did all he could to accommodate the new-found tolerance of the era. This was entirely in keeping with his great sympathy for the human longings and aspirations of a much-changed world situation.

The Bishop was on most of the Committees dealing with the Relations of Canterbury Province with the new United Churches abroad. He strongly supported the Church of South India, despite many criticisms levelled at its policy of allowing non-episcopally ordained ministers from abroad to be ministers of the CSI in the early stages. To-day, some thirty years later, the very strong position of the CSI shows clearly that Dr. Mortimer's judgement was right.

The Bishop was himself a member of the Joint Commission which prepared the *Report on the Relations between the Anglican and Presbyterian Churches* and was very pleased when the Anglican Chairman of this body, the Bishop of Derby, stood down to allow Dr. Mortimer to present the Report to Convocation on May 22nd 1957. The Commission had proposed that as a first step towards unity the Presbyterians (including the Church of Scotland) should replace the annually-elected Moderators of their local Presbyteries by Bishops, properly consecrated by Anglican Bishops. Such Bishops-in-Presbytery would permanently preside over their particular Presbyteries until they came to retire. The Anglicans, on their side, would take into their system the ordained "lay" elders who played an important part in the Presbyterian Churches. Unfortunately these plans were rejected by the General Assembly of the Church of Scotland and so did not materialise. Although the Scottish representatives on the Commission strongly supported the scheme, it seems that the historical associations of Bishops in Scotland in past centuries had made the whole concept of Bishops repugnant to the Scots, added to which the acceptance of bishops by the Church of Scotland seems to have been regarded as an unpardonable concession to England! Even the *Scottish Daily Express* came out against the idea. None the less the Report embodied a noble idea which might yet bear fruit in future years.

Dr. Mortimer supported the Scheme for the United Church of Lanka (Ceylon); he entered a technical objection to the proposed Church of North India and Pakistan in 1962 on the grounds that in the Unification Rite the 'ordaining' Bishop, though in fact a Bishop, would only be acting as a Presbyter. But his objection here was overruled by Convocation.

The Bishop's greatest interest in this field, however, was undoubtedly in the Anglican-Methodist Unity Scheme. He was not a member of the Anglican-Methodist Unity Commission whose Final Report, setting out the Scheme, was presented to Convocation in May 1968, but he was appointed Chairman of the Joint Committee charged by Convocation to examine the practical possibilities of the Scheme, which envisaged the attainment of organic unity between the two Churches in two distinct stages. In Stage 1, which was to take place as soon as possible, Anglican

Bishops and leading Methodist ministers were to lay hands on all the clergy of both churches, as far as possible, at a Service of Reconciliation, after which Methodist Bishops would be consecrated by the Anglican Bishops. These Methodist Bishops would ordain all future Methodist ministers. All the ministers would then be regarded as episcopally ordained, so that they could celebrate Holy Communion in churches of either denomination. Likewise the laity, whether Anglican or Methodist, could receive Communion in the churches of both denominations.

However it was felt that full organic union of the two Churches would have to be postponed until Stage 2, which might not take place for many years. This was on account of acute difficulties, such as the Methodists' determination to remain permanently in full communion with the other Free Church denominations and the Anglican system of patrons appointing clergy to lifelong freehold benefices, which could not be solved for a very long time. So until agreement on Stage 2 was reached the two Churches would continue to operate separately, each with its own set of Bishops.

Dr. Mortimer was most enthusiastic about the Scheme, and in his speeches made very generous concessions to the Methodists. He did not consider that differences in the doctrine of the Eucharist held by the two Churches were a serious obstacle, and although he was very worried about the Methodists' use of unfermented wine at the Holy Communion, this did not deter him from giving his full support. He was quite agreeable to Confirmation in the Methodist Church being by the circuit minister rather than the Bishop. It fell to him to move the three resolutions at a joint meeting of Canterbury and York Convocations on May 6th 1969 to the effect that the Scheme was theologically sound. The Methodist Church gave its full approval to Stage 1 and Dr. Mortimer cherished high hopes that at the joint session of Canterbury and York Convocations on July 8th 1969 the plan to go ahead with Stage 1 would receive the necessary 75% vote. However only 69.6% of the members voted in favour, so to the Bishop's great sorrow the Scheme had to be abandoned for the time being.

An important factor in the rejection of the plan was that in between the May and July meetings over a third of the clergy in the Dioceses had voted against the Scheme. Some of these doubtless had misgivings about postponing the greatest difficulties indefinitely until Stage 2, while others feared that the Service of Reconciliation would not in fact confer episcopal ordination on the Methodist ministers. Possibly, too, there was a feeling that union was being forced too quickly and that insufficient time was being given for the working of the Holy Spirit.

A case where the Bishop's views were not accepted by the majority arose in Full Synod on October 12th 1955 in the debate on the Report on the Archbishop's Commission on Nullity. Dr. Mortimer found the Report "extremely disappointing." In a long and eloquent speech he made a number of rather academic criticisms on minor points in the document, but what really disturbed him was the Commission's strong opposition to any kind of ecclesiastical tribunal to deal with cases of nullity, and cases of divorce where marriages were unconsummated. The Commission felt that such tribunals would be difficult to staff adequately and very expensive to run. The Bishop felt otherwise, partly because of his flair for legislation and partly, perhaps, out of his admiration for the centuries-old Roman Catholic system of tribunals for dealing with such cases. But the Archbishop likened Dr. Mortimer's speech to "being at Oxford again and listening to a tutor going through an essay.... It was a charming atmosphere but not very closely related to practical realities."

The Bishop showed himself to be far less conservative than often thought when the Liturgical Commission's Revised Baptism and Confirmation Services came before the Full Synod on January 20th 1960. There was much criticism from the Archdeacon of London and others that the new services were not conservative enough. Dr. Mortimer responded that he felt sorry for the members of the Liturgical Commission; they had spent much time and care in preparing the services and now had to listen to so much undeserved criticism. It was difficult to judge services which one had not heard performed. He had not heard them, but he welcomed the Commission's decision to embark upon a radical rather than a conservative revision. When the Series 2 services were later approved the Bishop gave them every encouragement in the Diocese and very soon declared that all Confirmations should be according to the Series 2 rite.

On May 1st 1961 Dr. Fisher attended the Upper House for the last time before his retirement from the Archbishopric, and the Bishop of London, Dr. Wand, who could not be present, asked Dr. Mortimer to give the farewell address. In a witty and amusing speech the Bishop stressed that the Archbishop's energy and administrative genius had been of immense value in 'rebuilding' the Church of England after it had emerged from the War financially impoverished and with its central machinery old and creaky. Like Queen Elizabeth I he had been brought to the kingdom at a particular time for a particular purpose. Dr. Fisher was delighted with the address, and wrote to Dr. Mortimer just afterwards; "Ever since you joined the Bishops' Bench I have been profoundly grateful to you for all that you have done, both to steady our steps and my steps in particular, and to give encouragement when it was often hard to find the straight and narrow path. It has meant more to me than you may have known."

The Bishop of Exeter was Chairman of the Joint Committee which produced the Report "Ought Suicide to be a Crime?" presented to Convocation on October 9th 1962. The Committee was set up when the Archbishop had received a letter from a distinguished coroner, who had been horrified to hear that the form of service used at the Burial of a suicide depended on whether or not the words "while of unsound mind" were added to the coroner's verdict. Many coroners, he said, did not realise this. The problem would not often arise nowadays, since inquests are usually adjourned until after the funeral has taken place, but in 1961 the Burial Service was sometimes denied to suicides who were not adjudged to have been of unsound mind at the time.

The Report was presented by the Bishop of Guildford, Dr. Reindorp, as Dr. Mortimer was abroad. It declared unequivocally that the Church regarded suicide as a grievous sin. At the same time in the Burial Service the Church was not condemning the soul to eternal punishment but commending it to God's mercy. The Committee felt that the Prayer Book Burial Service was not suitable for suicides, since it seemed to presuppose that the person being buried had died in a state of grace, whereas a suicide, as far as they could judge, had died in a state of unremitted sin. A suitable form of service for a suicide was therefore appended to the Report. It was very similar in structure to the Burial Service but it had a different Committal prayer and certain other modifications.

In the Church Assembly (and after 1969 in the General Synod) the Bishop's speeches were infrequent, partly because he preferred doctrinal and liturgical issues to the more mundane matters discussed in the Assembly, and partly because the long queue of speakers discouraged him from taking the floor. In November 1950 he defended the Assembly's Social and Industrial Commission's Report "Gambling, an Ethical Discussion" against many speakers, including the Bishops of London and Winchester, who claimed that it did not fairly represent the views of the Church of England. The Report took the view, very similar to Dr. Mortimer's, that gambling was permissible as an amusement, but became indefensible and indeed dangerous when it ceased to be such. The Assembly finally gave a qualified approval to the document, declaring it not to be fully representative of the mind and conscience of the Church of England as a whole.

In November 1957 Dr. Mortimer and the Bishop of St. Albans (Dr. Gresford Jones) jointly moved that the Assembly give its general approval to the recommendations relating to homosexuality contained in the Wolfenden Report. The main point in the Report was that homosexual acts committed by consenting adults in private should no longer be a criminal offence. The Assembly was deeply divided on this matter, and although the resolution had Dr. Fisher's support it was only carried by 155 votes to 138. Dr. Mortimer argued that the criminal law was not entirely consistent and had its medieval relics, of which the law on homosexuality was one. Adultery was a serious sin but equally it should not be a crime. The Report's recommendations would lessen the danger of blackmail. In some cases the law acted as a positive incitement to these practices rather than as a deterrent. There was no suggestion that they were condoning such conduct; they were all united in their disgust and condemnation.

As on divorce legislation, some felt that the Bishop's attitude on this matter was ambivalent. On the one hand he insisted that such conduct was repulsive, yet on the other hand he seemed to wish to make things easier for those who practised it! The explanation lay in the Bishop's deep sense of compassion - here was a tragic human situation and he wished to relieve the habitual homosexual offender, who could not rid himself of the weakness, of the suffering which inevitably followed. The following month the same matter was considered by the House of Lords; without making a major speech on that occasion, Dr. Mortimer took the same line and was happy later to see homosexual offences between consenting adults in private removed from the list of crimes. On March 7th 1958, before the legislation had passed the Commons, the Bishop was one of a number of distinguished signatories, including Lord Attlee, J.B. Priestley, Sir Julian Huxley and A.J. Ayer, who wrote to *The Times:* "The present law (on homosexuality) is clearly no longer representative of either Christian or liberal opinion in this country," and urged the Government to carry through the reform.

Another notable speech to the Assembly was given by Dr. Mortimer on February 18th 1965 before the voting on certain recommendations concerning Crown appointments which arose from the Howick Commission's Report. The Report had recommended that in the choice of suffragan bishops the two Archbishops, acting on behalf of the whole Church, should submit one name only to the Crown in consultation with the Diocesan Bishop concerned. But Dr. Mortimer, moving an amendment, argued quite passionately that the one name submitted should be chosen jointly by the Archbishop of the Province and the Diocesan Bishop involved. He pointed out that in recent years there had been an increasing tendency to recruit Diocesan Bishops from the ranks of the suffragans. There was therefore the possibility that if the two Archbishops wished a particular priest to serve on the episcopal bench they would first make him a suffragan for a trial run! The appointment of a suffragan was much more a diocesan than a provincial matter, Dr. Mortimer claimed. He was probably voicing here the disquiet of many Diocesans at the difficulty they have, as already mentioned, in choosing the team they want for the job.

Dr. Mortimer won his amendment, and to this day suffragan bishops are still appointed by the time-honoured procedure of the Diocesan submitting two names to the Crown, the first of which is normally chosen. This is despite the fact that Diocesan Bishops are chosen to-day in a completely different manner from in the past.

The Bishop accomplished much work for the Assembly through its committees and commissions. He was a member of the Church and State Commission appointed by the Assembly in June 1949, of which Sir Walter Moberly was the Chairman and Mr. (later Sir) John Guillum Scott Secretary. Its charge was to examine the whole relationship between Church and State in the Establishment and to report on any changes which seemed necessary. Dr. Mortimer contributed a great deal of the thinking behind the Commission's Report and was an admirable foil to the more Erastian ideas of Professor Norman Sykes.

The Report, published in 1952, recommended that there should be no Disestablishment at present, particularly as this would be regarded abroad as the dellberate repudiation of a continuous Christian tradition by the British people. At the same time the nature of the Establishment should be modified in some respects, and, with certain safeguards, power should be given to the Church, on the lines of Draft Canon XIII, to make optional and experimental deviations from the forms of worship prescibed in the Book of Common Prayer. The last point has, of course, been almost exactly fulfilled in the approval of the Series 1, 2 and 3 services.

As regards the appointment of Bishops, the Commission recommended that there should be no attempt to diminish the personal responsibility of the Prime Minister for the advice which he gave to the King. But if the Archbishops thought it desirable, a small committee should be set up by them in consultation with the Church Assembly's Standing Committee. It should comprise three Bishops, three clergymen and three laymen, who need not be members of the Assembly. When a vacancy in a see occurred this body, after conferring with representatives of the diocese concerned, should consult with and advise the Archbishops on the most suitable person to fill the see. A committee of this type was finally set up in 1977 with considerably greater powers than those recommended by the Moberly Commission. It submits one name to the Premier, and there is the feeling that this name should be accepted unless there are strong reasons to the contrary.

The Commission also recommended that a final Court of Appeal for Church cases should be set up, to replace the purely secular Judicial Committee of the Privy Council as the last Court of Appeal in such matters. The new Court should have one of the Archbishops as Chairman, sitting with two Church of England communicants who held, or had held, high judicial office. However, no change has been made in the law on this point.

In 1953 Dr. Mortimer was appointed by the Assembly to the Fees and Faculties Commission and became its Chairman in 1955 when Bishop Leeson had to withdraw owing to ill-health. The Commission was to take a fresh look at the whole system of payment of fees in the Church, especially as regards the need for, and reimbursement of, lawyers. It was also to examine the long-standing system of the Chancellor issuing Faculties to allow changes in the fabric of churches to be carried out. These were important questions, for critics of the Church of England often claimed that far too much of the Church's precious funds was spent on legal fees and argued that there was no more need for the regular services of lawyers in the Church of England than in the Free Churches. The Nonconformist bodies only employed lawyers when specific legal problems arose, whereas in the Church of England most of the high legal costs went to cover fees for the deeds of Institution of clergymen to livings, Letters of Orders (confirming the admission of men to deacon's and priest's Orders), Faculties and other routine procedures.

This Commission was something of an Exeter affair, since apart from Dr. Mortimer the fifteen members also included the Chancellor of Exeter Diocese, Mr. W.S. Wigglesworth, and the Diocesan Registrar Mr. (later Sir Godwin) Michelmore! All three were opposed to change generally in such matters, and several critics claimed that the Report was on this account far too conservative. None the less the Report, which was published in 1959, led fairly quickly to the 1964 Faculty Jurisdiction Measures and more recently to proposals about the remuneration of the Church's legal officers.

The Commission decided that the work of the Church's legal officers was in general necessary, since documents such as Faculties and Letters of Orders must be properly executed legal documents to avoid uncertainty. They considered that the remuneration of the Church's lawyers was low for the work done, but they favoured the retention of the existing system of fixed fees for each legal document or transaction, rather than paying the lawyers a salary. They felt that the Faculty system should also be retained, so should the system of parish fees for weddings, funerals and the like. The Church Commissioners' standard table of fees for these services should apply in every parish and should be revised more than once in ten years, as was the rule at the time. There was a Minority Report from six of the members who felt that Church lawyers should be paid a salary rather than fees.

At Dr. Mortimer's last appearance at Canterbury Convocation in May 1973 the President, Dr. Ramsey, said that throughout Dr. Mortimer's 24 years in the Upper House no-one had given more to Convocation than he had by his knowledge, wisdom, his diligence in counsel, and his belief in the service which the Convocations were able to render to the Church.

CHAPTER XIII

The House of Lords and Government Committees

Membership of the House of Lords is restricted to the two Archbishops, the Bishops of London, Durham and Winchester and the twenty one other Diocesan Bishops who are most senior by their date of appointment. Dr. Mortimer had been Bishop of Exeter for six years before he was introduced to the House on November 16th 1955 by the Bishops of Derby and Bath and Wells. His maiden speech, on May 17th 1956, was on the unexpected topic of postage stamps. Viscount Elibank had pointed out that since the War most countries had issued a number of attractive pictorial stamps each year to commemorate special events, but Great Britain continued to issue the same kind of stamps as in pre-war days. Dr. Mortimer strongly supported Lord Elibank; we could no longer live in the 19th century and British stamps should bear some indications of the splendour and history of our land. Very soon, of course, this policy was adopted.

In the House of Lords Dr. Mortimer rarely spoke on the wider aspects of home and foreign policy, but specialised in problems of human behaviour and human dignity on which he had expert knowledge. The Bishop of London, Dr. Ellison, in a broadcast in November 1977, said that in his judgement Dr. Mortimer and Dr. Ian Ramsey (late Bishop of Durham) had made more expert contributions to House of Lords debates than any other Bishops of their day. It is fairly certain that no other Bishop could surpass Dr. Mortimer in this respect, having regard to his seventeen years' membership of the House.

The first major issue to attract Dr. Mortimer's attention was the Bill for the Abolition of the Death Penalty, which was debated in July 1956. There was a sharp clash of opinions on this Bill after the Marquess of Salisbury had announced that the Government were allowing a free vote. Even Dr. Mortimer said that five years ago he would have voted against the Bill; traditional Christian ethics had always allowed the taking of life by the community as the most extreme form of punishment.

Since then, however, he had changed his mind on several grounds. There was public unease that some persons were hanged for murders for which they were not fully responsible, or for murders which were not premeditated. If there were different gradations of murder, with different penalties, much of this unease would be removed. But as he understood it this course was not possible, so he had to vote for abolition. (In fact, of course, capital and non-capital degrees of murder were later legalised for a few years before the death penalty for murder was finally abolished). Another reason was that the death penalty created a certain morbid excitment which was bad for morals in general. He considered that the death penalty depreciated in the mind of the ordinary man the sanctity of human life.

The two Archbishops and many Bishops voted for the Bill although the Bishop of Rochester, Dr. Chavasse, was strongly in favour of retaining the death penalty. On that occasion the Abolition Bill was defeated in the Lords, but it was discussed again on November 9th 1961, following the publication of the Home Office Report "Murder". This time Dr. Mortimer was even more strongly opposed to the death penalty. The spectacle of the State, with all the solemn majesty of the law, actually taking life in cold blood, sowed a seed of doubt in everyone's mind, a doubt whether human life was sacred after all, he said.

The Bishop was very pleased when the death penalty was abolished, for five years in the first instance, in 1965. In December 1969 the question of extending Abolition beyond five years came before the House of Lords. Dr. Mortimer again spoke in favour of Abolition though he was cautious enough to vote for Viscount Dilhorne's amendment that abolition be continued until 1973 rather than permanently. However the amendment was defeated and abolition of the death penalty for murder became permanent.

Reference to the Bishop's support for the Wolfenden proposals, as they affected homosexuality, in both the House of Lords and the Church Assembly has already been made. The Wolfenden Committee's full title was the Committee on Homosexual Offences and Prostitution, however, and the Bishop spoke on both problems in Parliament. In May 1959 the Street Offences Bill, which took a tougher line against prostitutes, came before the Lords for its second reading. While the Bishop supported the Bill on the whole, he objected to the term "common prostitute". If once a woman had been convicted for soliciting, the next time she was brought to court she was accused of soliciting "being a common prostitute". Such a description inevitably caused bias in the magistrate's mind, Dr. Mortimer said. Furthermore the expression inevitably implied that "once a prostitute, always a prostitute," which was neither fair nor just. Despite the Bishop's plea, however, the Bill became law on July 16th 1959 with the offending phrase still standing.

Another major concern of Dr. Mortimer's was the Abortion Bill, which came before the House of Lords in 1965 and 1966. The Bill greatly widened the grounds on account of which an abortion could be legally carried out. If two doctors certified in writing to this effect, pregnancy could be terminated for serious risk to the mother's life or grave injury to her physical or mental health, or for the possibility that the child's physical or mental health might be so affected as to deprive it of any prospect of "reasonable enjoyment of life", or if the mother was or would be mentally inadequate to be mother of the child. Lastly abortion would be allowed where the woman was mentally defective, or became pregnant when under 16, or became pregnant as the result of rape. Dr. Mortimer was very uneasy about any of these grounds being allowed, except where the mother's physical or mental health was in serious danger. He said that the vital point was the value which was placed on the foetus, a potential human life. Some speakers seemed to say that any pregnant woman should be entitled to abortion on demand, simply because she did not wish to bring her child to birth. Once one abandoned the principle that the mother's health must be at serious risk, this was the logical conclusion and it was a conclusion which the Bishop totally rejected.

Although the last clause, dealing with mentally defective women, girls under 16 and cases of rape, was completely eliminated from the Bill, the rest of the provisions became law on April 27th 1968. As a result there was a staggering increase in the number of legal abortions, which rose from 35,000 in 1967 to 166,000 in 1973. So many foreign women came to England for abortions that London became known as "the Abortion capital of the world." The number has fallen to about 130,000 a year now, of which 100,000 involve British women. In the first ten years of the Act there have been more than a million abortions in England and Wales, and abuses have been manifold. So it seems that Dr. Mortimer's fears were well founded.

The Bishop's major achievement in Parliament was undoubtedly his important part in securing a radical reform in the Divorce Law, which completely changed the situation regarding divorces in this country. In some ways these reforms had their origin in the Report of the Royal Commission on Marriage and Divorce published in March 1956. This had proposed new grounds for divorce and had raised the question whether one such ground should be the irretrievable breakdown of marriage. It was perhaps with this Report in mind that in January 1964 the Archbishop of Canterbury, Dr. Ramsey, set up a Commission, with Dr. Mortimer as Chairman, to re-examine the Divorce Law and to recommend any necessary changes. The Commission of fifteen included Lord Devlin, the Rt. Hon. E.W. Short, Viscount Colville of Culross, Lady Oppenheimer, Professor (now Sir) J.N.D. Anderson and Mr. Justice Phillimore. It met eighteen times and received much evidence, including advice from several judges, before publishing its Report "Putting Asunder: A Divorce Law for Contemporary Society" in July 1966.

The all-important point in the Report was that the sole ground for divorce in future should be the irretrievable breakdown of marriage. While the latter phrase had been borrowed from the Royal Commission's findings, the Royal Commission had suggested it as one of several legal grounds for divorce - it was quite a different matter to make it the only ground. A divorce trial, the Report said, would in some ways be analogous to a coroner's inquest - it would be a judicial enquiry into the alleged fact and the causes of the 'death' of the marriage relationship. The

Commission placed a duty on the court to adjourn a hearing if it was not satisfied that the possibilities of reconciliation had been exhausted. A decree should be witheld until the court was satisfied that financial provision had been made for the dependent spouse and any children of the marriage.

The Times regarded the Report as one of the most controversial of its kind ever written, which could well lead to allegations that the Church of England was setting double standards if not actually facing both ways! For while the Church would continue to impose the usual discipline on any of her members who remarried after divorce, it seemed as if divorce was going to be made considerably easier for non-churchmen! In answer to this the Commission insisted that they were concerned solely with the secular side of marriage and that the Report gave advice to the secular society on the secular law.

However the Report was acclaimed by both the Convocations and was recommended by the House of Lords to the Law Commission for further study as to its legal implications. There were indeed some serious legal difficulties. The Commission intended the divorce hearing to be an exhaustive enquiry as to whether the marriage had really broken down beyond all hope of repair; only in this case was a divorce to be granted. But lawyers felt that "irretrievable breakdown", however sound a concept in theory, was untriable. A marital offence, such as alleged adultery, either did or did not happen, but it would be very difficult to establish in court whether a marriage really was broken beyond all repair. An even greater objection was the time the new procedure would take in the divorce courts. In 1966 most divorce cases were undefended, many being but thinly-veiled cases of divorce by consent, and only took a few minutes to hear in court. But now it seemed that there would be a lengthy investigation in each case.

That autumn the Law Commission's Report came before Parliament and in a brilliant speech in the House of Lords on November 23rd 1966 the Bishop seemed to create order out of chaos and received strong support. The Divorce Law at the time, of course, required a matrimonial offence, such as adultery, desertion, or cruelty to be proved before the divorce could be granted. The divorce was then awarded against the person committing the offence, who was described as the "guilty party." The Bishop was quick to point out that the Law Commission's Report was in full agreement with "Putting Asunder" in regarding this present divorce law, based on the matrimonial offence, as completely unsatisfactory. It often caused great bitterness between the two parties when one of them, anxious to establish the matrimonial offence, described the other's conduct, through counsel and in the witness box, in most unpleasant terms. Even the courts in practice, he said, were more and more acting not on the offence itself, but on the ground that the marriage had irretrievably broken down.

If divorce by consent were to be introduced as an alternative, the Bishop continued, what would the marriage vows really amount to: "Till death us do part or when both decide to call it a day?" This remark brought cheers. Summing up, Dr. Mortimer ended, "I believe that public opinion, on the whole, now agrees that our divorce laws should be more realistic, decent and humane; that it does not want easier divorce, but it does want more sensible divorce . . . . In a word that the time has come to move away from our present miserable system, with all the bitterness it unnecessarily engenders, in the direction of something more civilised and enlightened."

Within three years all the outstanding difficulties were overcome. The ruling factor seems to have been that all sides were agreed that the matrimonial offence should no longer be a ground for divorce. The "Putting Asunder" group began talks with the Law Commission with a view to transforming the ideals expressed in their Report into workable law. Mr. Leo Abse, Labour M.P. for Pontypool and himself a busy divorce lawyer, took up the cause with great enthusiasm, even though as a Jewish humanist his background was very different from Dr. Mortimer's. In July 1967 Mr. Abse called together some twenty Labour M.P.'s interested in the proposed new law and the movement rapidly gained impetus.

The Law Commission's plan was to eliminate

altogether the lengthy inquisition into the state of the marriage envisaged by the "Putting Asunder" group and to replace it by a simple declaration that the marriage had broken up. In general two years' separation if the divorce was undefended, or five years' separation where a defence had been entered, would be accepted as evidence of the irretrievable breakdown of the marriage, as would also behaviour which the other party could not be expected to endure.

From Dr. Mortimer's point of view this development was most unfortunate, since it opened up the way to easier divorce, which was the last thing that he had intended. The undefended divorce after two years' separation could amount in many cases to divorce by consent and threatened to open the floodgates. But by this time Dr. Mortimer had gone so far that, as a fellow-Diocesan put it, he had little standing ground to resist the alteration.

Mr. Abse had hoped that the Bill would be moved by the Government, but the official attitude was one of neutrality throughout. So he put it forward as a Private Member's Bill on October 25th 1966, but it did not reach a second reading. On November 29th 1967 Mr. William Wilson, M.P. put forward a very similar Bill, which passed its second reading but had to be dropped for lack of time. Finally another Labour M.P., Mr. Alec Jones, put the proposals forward a third time on November 27th 1968. The Bill passed its third reading in the Commons on June 13th 1969 and at its third reading in the House of Lords on October 13th 1969 it was passed without a division. Dr. Mortimer spoke with less enthusiasm than before, but said that the Bill would neither weaken the institution of marriage nor damage society.

So on November 22nd 1969 the Divorce Reform Bill received the Royal Assent. The new law has certainly removed much of the rancour from divorce cases and it is too early for a final judgement to be passed. But the number of divorces has greatly increased since the new laws came in force. As late as 1960 there were only 25,672 divorces in the year. By 1970, the last year of the old law, there were 70,575 and in the following year there were over 110,000. By 1976 there were 146,415 divorces, as against 356,000 marriages in the same year. Lord Hailsham has recently suggested that the Divorce Law should now remain as it is for some years, to enable its effect to be assessed. With the new law there has come much pressure from more liberal Anglicans to allow divorced parties to remarry in church, a development to which Dr. Mortimer remained strongly opposed all his life. Although a parish priest cannot be prevented from remarrying divorced parties in the Church of England, and some marriages of this kind are solemnised in church, the number is still relatively small.

As regards Government Committees, Bishop Mortimer specialised in the treatment of prisoners and other offenders. From the late 'fifties he was on the Advisory Council on the Treatment of Offenders, and was chairman of a group which produced an influential report recommending the end of preventive detention. He was appointed to the short-lived Royal Commission on the Penal System, and when this was disbanded in 1966 he became a member of the Advisory Council on the Penal System and was its Deputy Chairman until he retired in 1974. He was Chairman of a sub-committee which carried out a detailed study of detention centres and produced a valuable report. He was noted at the Home Office and in the Prison Service for his shrewd and balanced judgement as well as for his kindliness and long service.

The Bishop's attitude to these matters is shown by some of the speeches he made in the House of Lords. On July 31st 1956, after Lord Moynihan had drawn attention to shortcomings in our prisons, Dr. Mortimer had some strong words to say. Prison Governors and staff were frustrated by conditions in prisons and by the buildings themselves. The buildings were gaunt, ugly, beastly and repellent in every way. The sanitary conditions were degrading and there was a queer aroma in prisons which he thought came from the prisoners. It was wicked to place recidivists in the same building with persons on remand and first offenders. In another speech in the Lords on February 21st 1963, he said that if recent changes meant that the Home Office would have more money to spend, he hoped that the first step would be to remove that blot on Britain's culture and civilisation - the prison at Dartmoor. This remark drew cheers, though the prison still stands there, gaunt as ever! During the second reading of the Criminal Justice Bill in May 1961 he said he was glad that there was no provision to restore corporal punishment, which he would have opposed.

Further evidence of the Bishop's shrewd and realistic, yet very charitable attitude on prison questions can be seen in his lecture "Punishment in a Christian Society", which he gave to various organisations. The punishment of offences, he wrote, is conducive to the maintenance of order in society, and order in society is in accordance with God's will. A total absence of punishment would lead to chaos and would, in itself, be unjust. Neither is the imposition of punishment inconsistent with love and forgiveness. Punishment, to be effective, must have a retributive as well as reformative and a deterrent element, so it must be unpleasant. But the regime must remember that offenders are still human beings and must be treated as such. Regard must be had to their personal dignity and their right to receive consideration and justice. Some flicker of hope must be kept burning in them and they must be enabled to retain and deepen their self-respect - otherwise reform becomes impossible.

The Bishop of Chichester, the Rt. Rev. E.W. Kemp, points out that in some respects Dr. Mortimer was enabled to do far more than Dr. Kirk ever had the chance of doing. He was able to bring his training in Moral Theology and Canon Law to bear on practical questions in the life of Church and State. Very few have had Dr. Mortimer's knowledge in these fields, but even fewer have had the chance to put that knowledge to such good effect.

CHAPTER XIV

The Bishop's Special Church Interests

One of Dr. Mortimer's great interests was the Society of St. Francis - the Anglican Franciscan Order - of which he was Bishop-Protector from 1949-73. Like many Catholic Anglicans the Bishop had long been fascinated by the Church of England's Religious Orders which began to be founded, very much on the Roman Catholic pattern, from 1845 onwards as a result of the teaching of the Oxford Movement. Various small Brotherhoods based on the Franciscan rule arose in the Church of England but eventually they were all absorbed by the Society of St. Francis, which was founded in 1921 by Brother Douglas who became the Society's first Father Minister. For some thirty years the Mother House has been at Hilfield, Cerne Abbas, Dorset. The Brothers (or Friars) live under the Franciscan rule and conduct Parish Missions, Retreats and other conventions; they wear the familiar brown habit with a shining white girdle and are the Anglican counterpart of the Roman Catholic Order of Friars Minor.

In 1949 Dr. Mortimer succeeded the Bishop of Hereford, Dr. R.G. Parsons, as Bishop-Protector. This office is akin to that of Visitor in other Orders, but it is uniquely Franciscan and was given by St. Francis to Cardinal Ugolino, the great Bishop of Ostia who later became Pope Gregory IX. We are indebted to Brother David, S.S.F., Father Minister of the Society from 1958-73, and to Brother Denis, S.S.F. for the following details.

Dr. Mortimer's first task was to press for a radical revision of the Society's Constitution; although still small in numbers, the Brotherhood was at the time poised for a considerable expansion of its work. Father Algy Robertson, who as Father Guardian shared with Brother Douglas the administering of the Society, was an old friend of the Bishop's and said at the time: "Bob is one of the cleverest men in Europe, but he has got a very legal mind!" At this time the Protector was, to most of the Friars, a remote but splendid figure. When Brother Douglas and Father Algy both died within a short time the Friars, who were somewhat under shock from this unexpected shaking of their foundations, increasingly looked to Dr. Mortimer for help and guidance. The Bishop quickly formed the most friendly relationship with Brother David, who succeeded Brother Douglas as Minister, and was heard to say at a General Chapter, "David has been Joshua to Algy's Moses!"

From then on the Bishop became much less remote and enjoyed parties and the like if they did not last too long. Once when the mother of a newly-Professed Friar said: "**What** a gorgeous lunch! Is it for St. Francis, for my son or for me?" the Bishop remarked drily: "I rather think it's for me!"

Dr. Mortimer presided with superb dignity and grace at the Life Professions of the Friars. His Charges, though very short, were always memorable. "Please don't waste your time and energies doing things which ordinary members of the Established Church can do as well or better. Go where we don't go and where we are not invited. I would like to see you at work in two particular, and I believe neglected areas - Girls' Schools and centres of Communist influence."

The Bishop hated fuss and his replies to questions were immaculately brief. Once, after listening to the Father Guardian speak for an hour on three major problems, he said: "First question - No. Second question - well, I suppose, yes - though it does seem a little unfair doesn't it? And of course, the third question - yes!"

Dr. Mortimer enjoyed discussing moral issues, and once when hurrying away from a visit to the Dorset Friary to get to Lords (!) he was chased by a Friar who called out: "A doctor friend of mine would value your views on Vasectomy." "Of course," said the Bishop, getting out of the car, "I've got time for that."

Brother David remembers with great gratitude all the guidance and support given to him by their "very wise and kind" Protector during his twelve years as Father Minister. With all his tremendous commitments to the Diocese and the Church at large the Bishop never refused to be on hand to help, and regularly gave time at the Palace for advice and discussion of the community's plans. He was a tower of strength in times of difficulty. The only time he ever spoke sharply to Brother David was just before the latter's election as Father Minister. Brother David, who was "very fearful" of his proposed new responsibilities, telephoned the Bishop and asked his permission to withdraw. "I thought you knew what obedience was," was Dr. Mortimer's reply, and the receiver was firmly put down!

The Bishop, who because of his signature was known affectionately to the Friars as "Plus Robert", said to them at the end of his term of office: "During my time as your Protector the Society has grown astonishingly and there are now three Provinces of Europe, America and the Pacific, each with its own Protector. No one could possibly pretend that I have been a good Visitor - but I hope I may have been of some use as a Protector. Not interfering in the day-to-day life of the Friars, but at hand to advise, to suggest and indeed to counsel. Now as I resign my Office your active works need no comment from me. They are manifold. But may I counsel you to remember the prime purpose of your life together - to be quiet and to pray. Be still, then, and remember God."

Even after his retirement the Bishop retained his interest in the Franciscans and often stayed at their Alnmouth Priory, which was not far from his Cumbrian home. He was there for two days only a few months before he died. During his time as Protector he gave his full support to the Community of St. Clare (or Poor Clares), the Society's Second Order for women which was founded in 1950. A contemplative and enclosed Order, the Poor Clares have the one house at St. Mary's Convent, Freeland, Oxford, where the Bishop also presided at the Life Professions of the Sisters. At his death the Mother Superior, Sister Gwenda Mary, wrote: "We shall always think of him as Robert-our-Protector and his visits gave us great joy."

The help which the Bishop was able to give to the Franciscans was enhanced by his position as Chairman of the Advisory Council on the Relation of Bishops and Religious Communities, to give it its full name. On Bishop Kirk's death in 1954 Dr. Mortimer succeeded him as Chairman of the Council and remained in office until his retirement from his See. The Council advises Bishops about charters and rule of existing Communities and on the establishment of new ones, and gives the same kind of advice to Communities themselves and those wishing to found new ones. Much of its business is of a legal and constitutional nature; both in this side of the work and in the more pastoral aspects Dr. Mortimer seemed to be in his element. He was a splendid Chairman and his wit and assiduity enabled the Council to get through its work expeditiously and with the minimum of boredom.

There were two developments in particular during his term of office. The first was the inclusion of women on the Council, which had previously been an all-male preserve. Originally the nuns had wished it so, but the climate changed and the Mother Superiors corporately requested membership of the Council. After discussion it was decided that three Mother Superiors should be added to the Council's strength; they first attended a meeting on November 8th 1966. The second important development concerned the adaptation of community life to modern conditions, especially in view of the publication of the Vatican Council's decree *Perfectae Caritatis* on this subject: Fr. A.V. Longworth, C.R. wrote a memorandum on this which was discussed in April 1967. At this meeting the Bishop proposed that a Working Party be set up to examine the whole question of renewal in Religious Communities. In 1969 this Working Party, whose original members had been personally appointed by the Bishop, became a permanent body, the Consultative Committee for Anglican Religious Communities. During the Bishop's term of office new editions of the Advisory Council's well-known publications *Guide to the Religious Communities of the Anglican Communion* and *Directory of the Religious Life* were published in 1955 and 1957. We are indebted to Dom Augustine Morris, O.S.B., formerly Abbot of Nashdom, for this account.

Another of the Bishop's special interests was Exorcism. In November 1963, for example, Dr. Mortimer held a service of exorcism at a country house in South Devon at the request of the local vicar. After lengthy investigations the vicar had been "satisfied that there was some ghostly presence there." The occupants had complained of furniture being moved, and of seeing a white form pass through the house. For two months they had been afraid to sleep there. But after the Bishop's visit all appeared to be quiet. Some of the accounts in the popular press gave the impression that the Bishop had acted in a way which was centuries behind the times!

Nothing could have been further from the truth. There has been a remarkable return to occult practices and black magic in England of late, and even if most of this underground activity scarcely touches the surface, there are times when the Christian priest or minister is called in to advise or deal with the situation. It is essential that the Church should be able to act with real knowledge in such cases. A tragedy in 1975 in which a man killed his wife in a frenzy, after an all-night exorcism ceremony during which forty demons were said to be cast out of him, shows how dangerous it can be to minister in such circumstances without the necessary training and knowledge. Both an Anglican incumbent and a Free Church minister had taken part in this exorcism.

There can be little doubt that the so-called parapsychological phenomena have a real existence, whatever the explanation. For the Christian there is the problem that Christ widely used the language of demon-possession in healing illnesses, many of which seem explainable to-day in purely medical terms. From the start of his episcopate the Bishop had had reported to him strange happenings like the work of poltergeists, demon-possession and sacrificial acts with a sinister significance - on all of these his advice was sought. On receiving such enquiries the Bishop would think carefully, take the best possible advice and answer clearly and to the point. "Personally I have never seen or heard anything of this kind," he would say, "but I must listen to the evidence of those whose integrity is beyond reproach and whose judgement I respect."

Because of the Bishop's strong desire for accurate information in this field he decided in 1963 to set up a Commission to look into the matter of Exorcism. In his Foreword to the Commission's Report, published by S.P.C.K. in 1972, he wrote: "The general attitude in the

Church of England (in 1963) seemed to be to regard exorcism as an exercise in white magic or a survival of medieval superstition. It was seen as the purely negative action of expelling an evil force or cleansing an evil environment. Its positive aspect as an extension of the frontiers of Christ's Kingdom and a demonstration of the power of the Resurrection to overcome evil and replace it with good was overlooked."

The Commission was unusual in including two Roman Catholic priests, Fr. T. Corbishley, S.J. and Fr. J. Crehan, who gave excellent help. The Secretary was the Rev. Sir Patrick Ferguson-Davie, Bt. and the other members were Dom Robert Petitpierre, O.S.B. (an Anglican Benedictine, who edited the Report), the Rev. Dr. E.L. Mascall, the Rev. Dr. M.H.B. Joyce (consultant psychiatrist) and the Rev. Dr. W.D. Omand (formerly Vicar of Chideock, who had specialised in Exorcism). The second part of the Report was given to Services and Prayers for Exorcism and Blessing of a Place and of Persons, Laying-on of Hands and Anointing with Holy Oil for Sick People and the Blessing of Holy Water.

The other part of the Report, which attempted to give advice on Exorcism, pointed out that it was still practised by the Orthodox Church and in the new Baptismal rite of the Roman Catholic Church. It was unfortunate, however, that exorcism tended to be regarded as exclusively concerned with demonic "possession", a concept which as usually understood was "extremely dubious".

No exorcism should be carried out, the Report advised, until the family doctor and a competent psychiatrist had thoroughly examined the medical aspects of the illness. But there might still be a need for exorcism after these steps had been taken. If so, the exorcism should only be undertaken by a priest with experience in such matters, and the explicit permission of the Bishop should be required in every individual case. If exorcism was decided on, the utmost effort should be made to train the patient in the practice of the Christian life; if he was a churchman regular prayer, confession and communion should be normal. Frequent laying-on of hands, and if the patient was properly instructed, one administration of Holy

Unction, were probably advisable, and might well effect the cure rather than exorcism. After-care by the parish priest, under the guidance of the Bishop or his deputy, was vital. It was recommended that every Bishop should appoint a priest as diocesan exorcist, and that centres of training should be set up in each Province, if possible in collaboration with the Roman Catholic Church.

Several dioceses appointed exorcists as a result of the Report, but there have been no sweeping changes in this field; requests for exorcism are rare and it is a subject which leaves many questions unanswered. When the Commission was set up there was a good deal of scepticism, some of it from fellow-bishops. But Dr. Mortimer was undeterred and went ahead with his plans. After the Report had been published some of his former critics changed their mind and asked the Bishop for his advice.

This chapter would be incomplete without mention of the Bishop's association with Inter-Church Travel. Dr. Mortimer first acted as leader of one of this company's cruises in 1962. It was an ecumenical tour - the first of its kind - comprising clergy and people of Anglican, Roman Catholic and Protestant Churches making a pilgrimage in the steps of St. Paul and to the Holy Land. On later voyages the Bishop led some great gatherings of Ecumenists, including the late Archbishop James of Christoupolis, the late Fr. Tom Corbishley, S.J., Lord George MacLeod, Dean Edward Carpenter, Dom Philibert Zobel and many others.

During pilgrimages he addressed the assembled company at Jerusalem, Mt. Athos, Patmos, on the site of the Church Council of Ephesus and other famous locations. Here his classical training, quite apart from his theological knowledge, stood him in very good stead. At Ephesus, for instance, he gave a talk on the key-word **theotokos** (mother of God) which Christians had used of the Blessed Virgin Mary and which had been discussed at the Council of Ephesus (431 A.D.) on that very site! Dr. Mortimer excelled, too, in the speeches which he made when the group was received at the Vatican by Pope Paul, or at Istanbul by the Ecumenical Patriarch, or at Jerusalem by the assembled prelates of all the Churches there. At these times he was not only knowledgeable but very impressive. He spoke with great sincerity, as a prelate of the Church which was already at unity with the others in its common love of God and of truth. He made the British pilgrims proud of their own heritage and at the same time humbled in the presence of their hosts from other great Churches.

Mrs. Mortimer usually accompanied the Bishop on these journeys and herself lectured on Mater Magna, for example, as the ship sailed between Ephesus and Athens. Often too he was assisted on these cruises by the Bishop of Crediton and Canon Rice. A particularly impressive moment was at Jerusalem when the Bishop led the "Maundy Thursday Walk", starting at the Syrian Church of St. James, reputedly the site of the Last Supper. A Syrian priest read our Lord's Words of Institution, the British visitors repeated them in English, then the procession went on to the Garden of Gethsemane and into the Church of All Nations, where the Rock of Agony stands. Here Dr. Mortimer conducted the people's devotions in a wonderful, simple way and the worship concluded with the singing of "When I survey the wondrous Cross." Strange as it may seem he was sometimes overawed by these meetings with world Church leaders and at great Ecumenical receptions he would often seek advice from diocesan colleagues on what he ought to do!

The Bishop helped Inter-Church Travel in other ways too. He introduced to the company the late Arthur Lowry Cole, who was subsequently to save them from financial disaster. In 1963 he became Chairman of the company's ecumenical Advisory Council, and his great wisdom kept him firmly in this position until he died. Other members of the Council included the Archbishop of Thyateira and Lord MacLeod; its Secretary was (and is) Canon A.E. Payton to whom we are indebted for much of this information.

Dr. Mortimer also helped and advised Inter-Church Travel as an unofficial 'business consultant' and was invaluable to the company as it became part of the State-owned Thomas Cook Group and later as it in turn was taken over by the Midland Bank. No matter what the problem was - spiritual or academic, social or ecumenical, administrative or financial, the Bishop had an uncanny knack of coming in, very quietly and unobtrusively, with just the right advice!

CHAPTER XV

The World of Education

Among the Bishop's numerous serious interests, few lay nearer to his heart than the cause of Christian Education. He was undoubtedly more interested in the Independent sector than in the State system. He did not preside over the Diocesan Education Committee as Bishop Curzon had done; indeed he proclaimed publicly that work in the Diocese had gone so well that he had never found it necessary to attend a single meeting! Even so he was always ready to support the Committee and its officers and his wise advice given behind the scenes sometimes greatly lightened the burden of those holding the responsibility.

In 1949 the Diocesan Director of Religious Education was Preb. J.B. Griffin, a very able administrator who had done a magnificent job seeing through all the practical implications of the 1944 Education Act. By 1956, however, Fr. Griffin was stricken with lameness and had to resign. In his place the Bishop appointed the Rev. E.A. Sampson, who had been Assistant Director ever since coming to the Diocese from Cumberland in 1949. Prebendary Sampson remained Director until his retirement in 1977.

At the end of 1953 Prebendary Griffin reported that there were 74 Aided and 103 Controlled Church of England Schools in the Diocese. Only the Aided Schools, of course, were Church Schools in the full sense, but the Church authorities had to find half the cost of providing and maintaining the Aided School buildings. This was becoming an increasing burden on the Diocese, since great expenditure was often needed to bring the buildings up to the much-improved Government standards. Prebendary Griffin had to report that over the years ahead 29 Aided Schools would have to be closed down. In many cases, however, new schools would be built to replace two or more smaller schools, so that the overall picture was not without promise. The Diocesan Education Committee had agreed to provide £70,000 to assist in the provision and maintenance of Aided Schools.

In 1967 Prebendary Sampson reported that there were

now 62 Aided and 90 Controlled Schools. The reduction in numbers was really very modest when one remembers that many of the schools in the 1953 count had hopelessly inadequate buildings. Between 1952 and 1967 no less than £500,000 had been found by the Church as a whole to bring the school buildings up to modern standards. Fortunately the Church was now required to contribute only a third of the cost of school buildings; soon this was further reduced to a fifth and eventually to 15%. The Diocesan Education Committee also showed a strong concern for Voluntary Religious Education (mainly Sunday Schools) and Youth Work.

Dr. Mortimer was particularly concerned over the well-being of the Aided Schools; he was keen for the clergy to teach in Church Schools and did all he could to encourage this and to elicit support for the Schools. Often he visited them himself; he loved little children and was very good with them. During his time nine Aided Schools were moved to completely new buildings. He was pleased too at the foundation of the Cuthbert Mayne Secondary School in Torquay in 1972. This is an Aided School jointly owned by the Roman Catholic Diocese of Plymouth and a body of Trustees appointed by the Bishop of Exeter. The Anglican Church meets 25% of the Churches' share of the building costs and the Roman Catholic Church 75%. At least 25% of the places are given to Anglican children. In 1973 the School was reclassified as a Comprehensive.

Even in the Diocese the Bishop's interest in Independent Schools was very apparent. Almost immediately on his arrival he became a Governor of Kelly College, Tavistock. In 1961 he became Chairman and continued in office until he resigned the See. A Governor wrote: "These were difficult years for schools and parents, with increasing costs, new technologies to be taught, and changes in the standards but not in principles. The Governors were fortunate in having such a leader as Robert. His wisdom, foresight and human understanding were of immense value." The present Headmaster, Mr. D.W. Ball, had Dr. Mortimer as Chairman only for a year, but he remembers the Bishop as an admirable Chairman, whose experience, swift grasp of facts and faith in the new Headmaster, kept meetings short and to the point.   Kelly's standing amongst the Public Schools increased steadily during the Bishop's term of office.

Dr. Mortimer was also Chairman of West Bank School, a Church of England Girls' Boarding School which was originally at Bideford. He himself suggested that the School should move to the Manor House at Sidmouth when this became vacant in 1954 through the death of Colonel Balfour. For some years the school flourished in the beautiful house and grounds of the Manor, and Mrs. Mortimer was a part-time teacher there. The Bishop was very disappointed when the worsening economic situation led to the School's closure in 1971.

The Bishop showed a keen interest in the other Public Schools in Devon. At Blundell's he always conducted the annual Confirmation service and showed great interest in the School. He loved attending matches and other activities. He was equally well-known at Exeter School, of which he was an ex-officio Governor, and at St. Margaret's, the Exeter Girls' School which became a Woodard School in 1975 with his full encouragement.

Mention of the name Woodard reminds us that great as was the Bishop's work for Christian Education within the Diocese, his main work in this sphere was as Chairman of the Woodard Corporation, in which office his influence was felt throughout the length of England and Wales. The Corporation had been founded by Nathaniel Woodard, sometime Canon of Manchester Cathedral, who died in 1891 and was buried in the ground of Lancing College, the first and most famous of his schools. In founding the Corporation Woodard declared it to be his wish "that for all future time the Sons of Her Majesty's subjects should be taught, together with sound grammar learning, the fear and honour of Almighty God, the Father, the Son and the Holy Ghost, according to the doctrines of the Catholic Faith, as it is now set forth in the Book of Offices and Administration of the Sacraments of the Church of England."

While still at Oxford in 1948 Dr. Mortimer had of course become Provost of the Midland Division of the Woodard Schools, which at the time comprised Denstone,

Ellesmere and Worksop Colleges, Smallwood Manor (Denstone's Preparatory School) and the two Girls' Schools, St. Mary's and St. Anne's, Abbots Bromley (where Katherine Mortimer was to be a pupil) and St. Winifred's Llanfairfechan. We are indebted to Colonel H.H. Story, M.C., formerly Registrar of the Woodard Corporation, for his excellent account of Dr. Mortimer's work, the main points of which are given below.

The new Provost quickly endeared himself to his colleagues, not only for his intellectual gifts and deep human sympathy but also for his great missionary zeal. One of his first policies was to encourage Worksop and Ellesmere Colleges, which had junior departments within the main building, to establish separate Preparatory Schools. Within nine months of becoming Provost Dr. Mortimer had persuaded the Chapter to buy at an auction Ranby House, a commodious mansion situated near Retford. After some structural alterations and the addition of a chapel, this became Worksop College's Preparatory School, taking 105 boarders and 45 day boys. Recently this school, with its ample playing fields, has taken ten day girls as well.

Only a short time after Dr. Mortimer got the Chapter to buy a small thriving school near Shrewsbury which as Prestfeld Preparatory School became the Preparatory Department of Ellesmere, with 220 boys half of whom are boarders. Many of the Fellows of the Chapter were averse to buying it as it was largely a day school, and the Woodard Foundation had always taught that children were better educated within a resident community where religion was a living force. However Dr. Mortimer was able to persuade them that many middle-class parents, who strongly desired their children to receive a good moral and religious education, had been cruelly hit by taxation and inflation, such that they could no longer afford boarding school fees. At the same time Dr. Mortimer held that day boys should participate in organised games and many out-of-school activities, including Chapel worship on Sundays, which had previously been the preserve of boarders. This policy was most successful at Prestfeld and it was only later that extra boarding accommodation was provided.

When on becoming Bishop Dr. Mortimer decided he must resign as Provost, the eight Midland Division Schools all had waiting lists, despite increased fees. Staff salaries had been raised, school buildings had been improved and enlarged and married masters had been provided with houses within or near the school campus where possible. In his brief but invigorating reign, Dr. Mortimer had infused new life into the Division, attending every Chapter meeting and frequently taking services in the School Chapels.

When the Corporation's President, Dr. Kirk, died in 1954, Dr. Mortimer was the obvious choice as a successor and was admitted to the office on October 20th 1954, initially for a period of ten years. But on three occasions the Chapter pressed him to continue, so that he remained President for eighteen years to the day, resigning in October 1972. At the time he became President the Corporation comprised the Southern, Western, Northern and Midland Divisions. Each was managed independently by a Provost, Bursar and up to thirty Fellows. The Fellows were both individually and collectively responsible for the finances of their Divisions until these became limited companies in 1974. The President's job was to co-ordinate the affairs of the Divisions so that the Corporation could act as one body and speak with one voice.

The Bishop fulfilled this function admirably. He had little time for administration but his judgement was always apposite and his decisions unquestioned. While his lack of small talk kept him at a distance of others who stood in awe of him, his deep and warm human sympathy endeared him to all those who penetrated his reserve. His contributions to the policy of the Woodard Corporation were outstanding. A new Eastern Division was formed in 1968. The magnificent Chapel of Lancing College, which was begun in 1868 and built slowly as funds became available, is still not finished, but the west front was completed in Dr. Mortimer's time; it includes the largest rose window in England. The Corporation flourished generally and continued to expand; the Bishop brought his influence quietly to bear on every aspect of school government, emphasising that education of the mind was of little value unless it was encircled by an education which included morals and religion. Every school prospectus brought this point home clearly.

We have left rather late, perhaps, our account of the Bishop's work as Chairman of the Governors of his old school, St. Edward's, Oxford - a position which he was particularly proud to hold. A Governor of the School since 1947, he succeeded A.B. Emden as Chairman in 1951, when the Rev. H.E. Kendall was Warden. A close friendship grew up between the Bishop and Fr. Kendall; as we have seen the latter took a benefice in Exeter Diocese on his retirement from the School in 1954. He was succeeded as Warden by Mr. Francis Fisher, a son of Archbishop Lord Fisher. Mr. Fisher records that the Bishop's influence had a profound effect on his life and career: "Bob guided and helped me in a remarkable way . . . . He was, of course, a superb Chairman of a meeting - always concise, decisive, humourous and rapid! He never missed a meeting in my twelve years, and unlike some Headmasters I always looked forward to Governors' meetings! . . . . The Headmaster's job is a lonely one - he is called upon to make decisions endlessly throughout every day and this is a buck he cannot pass. Although he can seldom call on them he needs to know that there are friends to whom, in the end, he can go for support and advice. Bob, of course, never interfered. He was far too wise for that. He knew instinctively when to lend his support, and he knew too that the most valuable thing he could give was his friendship. I record now my very deep gratitude for all that he gave me."

The present Warden, Mr. Henry Christie, had Dr. Mortimer as his Chairman for seven years and was most impressed by him. "He worked exceedingly hard as School Chairman," Mr. Christie told us, "and it was noticeable that he knew everything that was going on." One evening the Bishop, along with some of the younger Governors, had coffee with some of the boys at the School. On first seeing Dr. Mortimer the boys thought that he must be "the old man" of the Governors and prepared for some dreary conversation! But they were surprised at the Bishop's keen interest and understanding. Afterwards the Bishop, who had been most challenging in his approach to the boys, said to the Warden, "They forget that you have children, you know."

An especially happy occasion was the School's Centenary celebrations in 1963. The Archbishop of Canterbury (Dr. Fisher), the Bishop of Oxford (Dr. H.J. Carpenter) and the Bishop of Ely (Dr. Noel Hudson, an old boy of the School) all attended, besides Dr. Mortimer, and it was a time of great rejoicing, particularly as the School had shown continuous expansion over those hundred years. The *History of St. Edward's School* commented: "It was no idle boast of Warden Fisher's, at Gaudy 1961, when he doubted if any school were better governed." Dr. Mortimer resigned the Chairmanship on his retirement, but remained a Governor until his death.

From 1955-69 Dr. Mortimer was also Chairman of Summer Fields, the Oxford Preparatory School where the Bishop's sons Mark and Edward were pupils. This school had been privately owned until 1955 when its joint Headmasters John Evans and Geoffrey Bolton decided to secure its future by making it a charitable trust. Just after the War when Mark was at the school, Professor Mortimer had already established a reputation in the Family Race, where he was a striking figure with his black stock flapping in the breeze as he sped rapidly down the course. By the time Edward arrived in 1951 his father was Bishop of Exeter and there were gaiters too doubling along! Dr. Mortimer also captained some celebrated cricket matches with Governors, masters and Old Summerfeldians in the teams. One of these was somewhat pretentiously described as "The Prime Minister's XI v. the Bishop of Exeter's XI". True, Mr. Macmillan did not actually play in the match, "his" XI being captained by the **Labour** M.P. Henry Usborne (an Old Summerfeldian) who stood in on his behalf! But the game was none the less entertaining for that.

Mr. P.M.B. Savage, Headmaster from 1960-75, declares that the appointment of the Bishop as Chairman of the brand-new Governing Body was an inspired choice. We have already given the Headmaster's description of Dr. Mortimer's exceptional ability as Chairman, although unlike the Warden of St. Edward's Mr. Savage did not feel that the Bishop was really at ease with the boys. Wherein lay the difference? It may have been a matter of the age of the boys. The Bishop as a long-standing University teacher had much in common with students and therefore with sixth forms. He also had a winning way with children. It may be, though, that he was not so well attuned to the ways of boys of ten and eleven years old. Mr. Savage adds, however, that Dr. Mortimer was in his element when presiding at a dinner at Claridge's to launch a School Appeal, and likewise at the School's Centenary Dinner at Balliol in 1964.

How far did the Bishop retain his interest in the Universities after moving to Exeter? A rather fascinating remark in his Obituary in *The Times* stated: "He was an ex officio member of the Court and Council of Exeter University, but took little part in the University's life: for him there was only one university, not even Oxford, but Christ Church." In fact the Bishop always kept a watchful eye on Exeter University after becoming Diocesan, although lack of time, especially in view of his substantial school commitments, prevented him from taking a very active part, especially in later years. He gave strong suppport to the building of the Mary Harris Chapel at the University in 1954, and was anxious that it should be a Church of England foundation. The appointment of the Lazenby Chaplain, a full-time Anglican Chaplain at the University, also owed much to his influence, and he strengthened the link between the Cathedral and the University by appointing as Chancellor the Rev. John Thurmer, who had previously held the Lazenby Chaplaincy. The Bishop also took a leading part in the negotiations through which the Cathedral Library came under the care of the Librarian of the University, and gave his strong support to the appointment of Canon J.R. Porter, who had gained Firsts in both History and Theology at Oxford and was then Chaplain of Oriel College, as the first full-time Professor of Theology at the University in 1962.

The Bishop retained to the end his deep personal attachment to Christ Church and frequently returned there, although as V.F.A. Mason noted,"he paid the penalty exacted from most of us in that fewer and fewer people knew him." Dr. Mortimer was appointed an Emeritus Student of Christ Church in 1950 and an Honorary Student in 1968.

Dr. Mortimer also had a deep affection for his own alma mater Keble College, of which he had been an Honorary Fellow since 1951. With his friend Mr. Dick Walters he founded in 1948 the celebrated "Apple Tree Dinner" which was held in the Senior Common Room at Keble in September each year. It was in effect an Annual Reunion of their closest Oxford friends, most of whom had been Keble undergraduates of the Bishop's own year. Robert always took the chair at the dinner and gave the toast "The Immortal Memory of the Apple Tree" - we have not elucidated the arcane reason for this unusual title! The idea was born when the Bishop and Mr. Walters met the Bursar of Keble, Mr. Vere Davidge, at the Universities' Cricket Match at Lord's in 1948 - the two friends attended this match each year. The dinner proved very popular from the outset and still goes on, though the numbers diminish year by year. Among the regular attenders were Mr. H.B.L. Wake (formerly Headmaster of St. John's, Leatherhead), Mr. Russell Meiggs and Archdeacon Babington. The company were very sad in 1976 when the Bishop died only a few days before the dinner was due to take place.

The Bishop of Exeter is always Visitor of Exeter College, Oxford, which was founded in 1314 by a famous Bishop of Exeter, Walter Stapeldon. Though the Visitor's presence is only needed on rare occasions, Dr. Mortimer visited the college, preached in Chapel and was the guest of honour at dinner. Sir Kenneth Wheare, who was Rector of the College from 1957-72, also met Dr. Mortimer on various occasions when he presented candidates to the Bishop for Institution to livings in Exeter Diocese in the College's gift. When attending such Institutions Sir Kenneth, often accompanied by the Rev. Eric Kemp (Chaplain of the College and now Bishop of Chichester), enjoyed his visits to the Palace and was much impressed by Dr. Mortimer's addresses at these services, which showed a considerable knowledge of local history and the background of the parish.

CHAPTER XVI

The Bishop's Later Writings

In 1950, just over a year after his Enthronement, Dr. Mortimer published his well-known volume *Christian Ethics* under the Editorship of Professor E.O. James in Hutchinson's University Library series. A work of 138 pages, it contains no Foreword or Preface. It appears to be addressed to the more intellectual reader but not so much, perhaps, to the professional theologian. A note on the dust jacket says that it is a discussion of the general ideas which underlie Christian ethical teaching, treating of such subjects as conscience, the concepts of sin and virtue and the relation between morality and religion. The note adds that the book also attempts to explain the traditional Christian attitude towards certain matters of conduct such as marriage and divorce, gambling and the rights and duties of private property. The final chapter, which is not included in this summary, is entitled "The Sanctity of Human Life" and deals with such topics as the just war, suicide, capital punishment and the restrictions on the right to kill in war or in self-defence.

The book was quite unlike most modern works on Christian Ethics, which attempt to produce Christian solutions to a wide range of personal, social and political moral problems. Dr. Mortimer only covered a few problems of this kind in the book, being largely guided in his choice by the topics, such as Marriage and Divorce and Gambling, on which he himself had specialised knowledge. The book might be regarded, in fact, as a more popular exposition of some of the basic ideas in *The Elements of Moral Theology*. Thus the first three chapters are entitled "The Bible and Ethics", "Authority and Conscience" and "The Duty of Religion", and on p.48 he states: "It is not its purpose (sc. the purpose of Christian Ethics) to lay down a number of rules as God's commandments and require men to conform to them. Its aim goes far beyond this. The pattern of behaviour which it describes, the obedience to conscience which it demands are only steps towards the creation of a character. And that character presupposes and requires a constant dependency upon God. Ethics without prayer tends towards self-sufficiency, complacency and pride." Much of Christian Ethics, then, consisted in the faithful discharge of one's religious duties. These included private prayer, simple rules of feast and fasts, almsgiving and above all attendance at the Eucharist. A good deal of Christian Ethics was therefore concerned with Ascetic theology and to Mortimer the two disciplines were quite inseparable.

A somewhat critical review of the book in *Theology* by Provost H.C.L. Heywood pointed out that no discussion of the epistemology of Christian Ethics was included, and claimed that the Bishop put his readers in an impossible dilemma when on the one hand they were told that Christians were "under moral obligation to obey the Church", but that on the other hand "conscience is always to be obeyed." The review went on to say: "The impression given by the frequent references to authority ('it is generally agreed', 'it is the general view', 'it is held by some people', 'the tradition forbids') is that of weakening any attempt to argue from the foundations."

However the review only showed how little the methods of traditional Moral Theology had penetrated the Church of England at the time! Most Anglicans of Catholic approach will readily understand how, while in any normal circumstances the Church must be obeyed, yet in the last resort the conscience of the individual Christian must always be the final arbiter. In Chapter 4, "The Duty of Obedience" for example, Dr. Mortimer begins: "It may, perhaps, seem strange to say that the first of our duties towards our neighbour is to obey the law." Later (p.65) he adds that though the obligation of human law upon conscience is essential to good government and stable society, yet there are rare cases when a man might feel in good conscience that his Christian duty was not to obey a very unjust or anti-Christian law.

The Bishop expressed his great concern (p.59) that at the time he wrote "In every branch of life there is a prevailing temper of disobedience.... Men are prepared to obey only where they understand, approve and like." This began in the home, "where the disobedience of children towards their parents is notorious" and had spread to every part of society. The Bishop was particularly anxious that the Canon Law should be revised, because the old Canon Law was too narrow and rigid for contemporary needs and for this reason it was widely ignored in practice. So the task of revising Canon Law was of national importance, "because on its success depends the beginning of a recovery of order and obedience within the Church. And that recovery would mean much for the renewal of the spirit of obedience throughout the nation." (p.61). Those words were written in 1950; thirty years or so later the Canon Law has been fully revised, yet there is even less sign of a widespread return to obedience as understood in earlier days!

In the last chapter the Bishop showed much sympathy with the pacifist; his case was "very plausible" and if its premiss (that modern war was more terrible than any tyranny) was accepted, moral theology would allow pacifism. Even so he retained a place for the just war and asserted that disarmament was certainly wrong, for it made resistance impossible whatever the rights of the case.

The book was too traditional to create a landslide and too short, perhaps, to be regarded as a weighty work. Yet in view of its unique approach for an Anglican work it was widely read.

In 1951 the Bishop's paperback *The Duties of a Churchman* was published as the first of the Lent Books issued by the Dacre Press (A. & C. Black). A short work of 78 pages, it had its origin in the *Exeter Diocesan Leaflet* articles (1949-50) on "The Spiritual Discipline of the Laity" already mentioned on page 70. The chapters of the book were based on the six rules of life set out in the 1948 Church Assembly Report on the duties and obligations involved in membership of the Church of England. The committee had been appointed at the request of the House of Laity.

The book had a very good sale and was reprinted in 1955. Despite its non-technical language the book is of great depth and precision in its teaching. The God-centredness of Mortimer's approach is shown by the following (p.30): "It is not the Church's first business to teach people the right way to live, nor to promote social justice, nor to be the instrument of founding and spreading God's Kingdom on earth. Her first business is to worship God, to glorify and praise Him. If Church-people play their full part in that activity, they learn in the course of it the right way to live, they come to demand social justice, they desire to imitate our Lord in His love for the poor and care of the sick, and so constitute in themselves the Kingdom of God, and by their influence and example extend that Kingdom." It was a memorable book and we quote *The Guardian's* reviewer: "There is no one more competent than Dr. Mortimer to produce a book of this kind. His commentary is lucid, vigorous and direct; it cannot but inspire confidence."

In 1953 another paperback by Mortimer, *Western Canon Law*, was published by A. & C. Black. This was a transcript of five lectures given to the Church Divinity School of the Pacific and the Law School of the University of California at Berkeley in the spring of 1951. The lectures were described as introductory, and were intended particularly for Anglican ordination candidates. Yet this book probably won more acclaim than *Christian Ethics*, if only because scarcely any other brief work on this subject existed in English, apart from the 1947 *Report of the Archbishops' Commission on Canon Law*. The first four chapters covered the history of Canon Law up to the time of the revision currently being undertaken by the Convocations. The last chapter was on the Characteristics of Canon Law, with special reference to the modern situation in the Church of England. The book only ran to 90 pages, yet it was a marvel of compression and, like all Mortimer's works, was very scholarly and lucid in its exposition.

The book attracted very favourable reviews, of which Sir Maurice Powicke's (J. Theol. Studies, 1954, p.150) is one of the best. Sir Maurice wrote: "His sense of practical duty, as a bishop who has studied and taught the history of canon law, has enabled him to give his lectures more 'actuality' than books of this kind usually possess .... He is hopeful of a revised form of Establishment in which a renewed and re-invigorated Church, 'speaking with the authority of the Body of Christ', will prove a willing and effective partner of the State. This conclusion is one of the strongest testimonies to the English capacity for compromise that I have ever read. It presents us, **inter alia,** with a picture of the House of Laity in the Church Assembly maintaining the 'immutable' parts of the canon law in a rapidly changing social system, and of almost incredibly tactful bishops dealing with hard cases with a casuistry derived from both deep spiritual insight and a subtle knowledge of the world. And yet the Bishop of Exeter may be right."

In retrospect after over twenty five years, it seems that far too great a spirit of lawlessness reigns to-day for such an ideal to be realised in the present century. Yet the book showed an unusual combination of a deep devotion to traditional Catholic teaching, a certain amount of Erastianism and yet a marked concern for human needs in a fast-changing society which was perhaps uniquely found in the mind of Robert Mortimer.

While this concludes our summary of the Bishop's books, it should be emphasized that a very important part of his writings were in the form of short articles or pamphlets. His articles in the *Exeter Diocesan Leaflet* which appeared nearly every month for 24 years maintained an astonishingly high quality for the whole of this time. If declining health caused a slight falling-off of the Bishop's effectiveness in certain fields over the last few years of his life, there is no sign of this in these articles, which showed their accustomed originality, scholarship, wisdom, humanity and common sense until the very end of his episcopate. There was often humour shown. In August 1950, for example, commenting on Rule 6 of the Report on the Spiritual Discipline of the Laity - "To seek a quiet conscience" - the Bishop noted: "When I first read this rule, I thought it must be a misprint. For surely what most of us need - and especially perhaps what regular church people need - is not a quiet conscience but an unquiet one."

In December 1950, when the Pope was proposing to proclaim the Assumption of the Blessed Virgin Mary as an official dogma of the Roman Church, the Bishop, quoting part of a Diocesan Conference address, wrote: "The belief is not in any way a novelty. It has been held by millions of Christians, and has been so held for centuries. It was widely held in England before the Reformation, as the dedication of a number of our churches clearly shows.... We are not called upon to deny or to seek to disprove the Assumption. There is no need to brand belief in it as heresy and deluded superstition. What we do deny is the necessity of this belief to salvation and the consequent condemnation as heretics of all who do not believe it. We hold rather that it is a pious opinion, which a man may accept or not accept without any question of his loyalty to Christ and of the sincerity and adequacy of his faith in the Incarnation. It is not a subject for dogmatizing. Let those who have this belief in the Assumption thank God that by means of it they are brought to a deeper love of our Lord and understanding of His Church, wherein they see His Mother pre-eminent in grace and beauty of holiness."

Not only in Exeter Diocese, but amongst a wider circle of Anglicans this statement was regarded as showing much wisdom and giving clarity to an issue which had caused considerable confusion in churchmen's minds.

Other articles covered subjects ranging from football pools or voting in General Elections to Judgement and the After-Life. "At this point I have to confess that I myself have never taken part in a football pool," the Bishop wrote in April 1951. "The reason is that I do not understand how they work. It appears that one must have an adequate grasp of permutations and combinations. But my admirable schoolmasters totally failed to overcome my crass stupidity in that matter." Dr. Mortimer was fascinated with the science of determining what was right and what was wrong for Christians. We emphasize the word "science", for the Bishop never spoke "off the cuff" on such matters - his opinions were always founded on much study and expertise.

Some of the articles were about diocesan clergy who had retired or died. Senior dignitaries such as Archdeacons nearly always received a "mention", but often incumbents of quite tiny parishes were remembered too. In the December 1966 *Leaflet*, amidst his busy Parliamentary activities, the Bishop wrote of the Rev. W.H. Smale (Rector of Petrockstowe from 1925-61): "He spoke the language of the people among whom he lived and whom he served. He identified himself with them and their lives. He was one of the last of the country parsons to farm his own glebe. He was said to be the best judge of sheep in his district. For all that he was, also, a good shepherd of his people." Such a priest was to Dr. Mortimer as important as any diocesan dignitary.

CHAPTER XVII

Eventide Years

It was at the Diocesan Synod on January 28th 1973 that Dr. Mortimer first announced his intention to resign the See on October 1st. The Bishop's countenance was sad and he looked tired as he broke the news. As is often the case when a man retires from an important position after many years' service, one could sense that Dr. Mortimer was torn apart emotionally by the situation. He loved the work of a Diocesan and would have given anything to be able to continue effectively as Bishop for another twenty years. But on the other hand he felt his physical strength and energy steadily slipping away with old age - he knew he could no longer do the work in the way that he would have wished.

He told the Synod that he was now 70 and it seemed a good time to retire. "I shall have been Bishop for $24\frac{1}{2}$ years. It is long enough. The Diocese needs a change, so with great sadness I shall leave. It has been a time of very great change and great interest for me. It is very difficult as yet to form a clear picture of what one has done or what one has not done. I think I have been wonderfully fortunate in the people I have selected to help me. They have been a marvellous team.

At my age I get frightfully tired very easily now. There are so many changes within the Church going on, and one becomes more conservative the older one becomes. Life within the Church is very vigorous and it needs younger people to lead it and direct it." The Bishop added that he had bought a house in Cumberland which should be ready for occupation by the autumn.

Those who knew Dr. Mortimer closely were probably not over-surprised at the announcement. For several years he had been finding the "night work", as he called it, a great strain. Night after night he would return from Institutions, Confirmations and other functions, often taking place in a far-flung corner of the Diocese, at any time between 10 p.m. and midnight. Sometimes returning home as the Cathedral clock struck 11 or 12 he would say to his Chaplain: "Home again safely, thank God. The Dean and Canons have all been tucked up in bed for hours, lucky chaps! That's what gets us in the end, the growing burden of night work. All the bishops say so, and they are right." "A reduced vitality appeared to trouble his later years," *The Times* commented, "in the midst of an exercise, meeting or debate, he would lose interest and extricate himself with no attempt at camouflage - and this with a suddenness which must surely have had some medical explanation." Sometimes during this period he looked very weary and poorly when preaching in Church.

None the less the Bishop tried hard to maintain, right to the last, the high standards of preaching and teaching for which his episcopate had been noted, and during his last few months in office he gave four magnificent addresses which summed up all the wisdom which he had accumulated during his 24 years as Bishop.

The first of these was given to the Diocesan Synod when he announced his forthcoming resignation. It was on the Permissive Society. One reason for the increase in crime and violence, the Bishop felt, was present-day affluence, which encouraged greed and envy. But deeper and more pernicious was the widespread revolt against authority. All the hitherto generally accepted moral judgements were questioned. When some school children rebelled against uniforms or classroom discipline, they were often supported and encouraged by their parents. Ideas that used to be universally accepted like "you don't steal, cheat or lie" are now barely respectable in wide circles, and sometimes one had to be quite brave even to mention them!

The picture was not all black, for there was an astonishing wealth of idealism among young people to-day, such as righteous indignation against cruelty and injustice, and a genuine compassion for the old, the lonely and the handicapped. The Church had some blame for the trouble, for she had over-reacted against the narrow, censorious attitude of Christians in the past, and was sometimes too ready to let every man be his own judge, apparently refusing to condemn anyone or anything.

In such a situation the Church should perhaps call a

halt to this kind of thing, and concentrate more on reaffirming her own moral standards and teaching. Christians themselves should be very careful not to show the materialism, greed and envy which they rightly condemned in the world. Parents should take every possible step to see that their children had the right kind of education. In parishes the utmost importance should be attached to the quality of the Sunday School.

The second address was given at the Bishop's Farewell Service for churchmen in the Plymouth area, at St. Andrew's, Plymouth in June that year. The Bishop preached on Isaiah 6, v.1. "I saw the Lord, high and lifted up and his train filled the temple." Whenever a man felt himself acutely in God's presence, he was filled with a sense of the otherness and awfulness of that which he had approached, and also of his own utter dependence, unworthiness. This sense of mystery and awe was the heart of worship, and worship was the heart of religion. Those who sought to denude religion and life of its mystery, who wished to set down in intelligible terms all that is known, and deny that there is more, were cutting themselves off from one never-failing source of life, aspiration and advance. Far happier were they to whom was given something of Isaiah's vision and who were able to cry from their heart: "Holy, holy, holy, Lord God of Hosts."

The third address, given at the Farewell Service at St. John's, Torquay the following month, also dealt with the all-important subject of worship and was on the text "Be still, and know that I am God." (Psalm 46, v.10). The modern age had become one of increasingly heavy activity; man was so busy about his earthly tasks that he had no time to think about God and the eternal values. Even churchmen tended to be drawn into the same whirlpool. Parish churches were often so much taken up with activities that there was no time to listen for "the still, small voice of God." Christians should find time during the day to spend some moments of quietness, reflecting on the beauty and majesty of Almighty God. There was probably nothing that man needed so much, to heal him of the bodily and spiritual ills of to-day, as time to listen to God's voice.

The last of these fine addresses was at the great

Eucharist at the Cathedral on July 18th 1973, when a packed congregation of clergy and laity came to give thanks for the Bishop's 24 years in the Diocese and to bid him farewell. Five Bishops, hundreds of clergy, civic dignitaries and leaders of organisations from all over Devon mingled with lay representatives from every parish in the Diocese. If sad, it was a splendid and dignified service. Trumpeters were present to acclaim the Bishop, who celebrated the Series I Eucharist, and glorious hymns were sung. The Bishop had the reputation of rising to a great occasion in his addresses and the people were not disappointed.

Choosing as his text St. Paul's farewell to the elders of the Ephesian Church at Miletus (Acts 20, v.32) the Bishop, quoting the Apostle's warning that "grievous wolves shall enter in among you, not sparing the flock," mentioned three dangers which confronted the Church at the present time.

First, there was a danger that changes in church worship might merely take the form of a trendy conformity with the passing fashions of each decade. It was right that worship should be made more meaningful, but that must not mean the easy informality of a saloon bar conversation. For the expression of its awe and reverence worship needed a special kind of language, a rich imagery and a majestic, poetic style. Make public worship too informal and it became insipid and meaningless.

Secondly, while he much welcomed the greater involvement of the laity in Church government, and hoped that laymen would in future take over the deacon's role of searching for "the sick, poor and impotent people of the parish," laymen could only play an effective part in Church government if they were adequately informed in theology and church history. So much more instruction for the laity was needed.

Thirdly the Bishop detected among the clergy "a certain disillusionment with the parochial ministry, a certain bewilderment and confusion as to what exactly they are supposed to be doing." With a few exceptions the clergy were terribly overworked and underpaid. Their wives, too, especially felt the strain. Many wives were forced to go out to work to make ends meet, and did a good deal of parish work too. There was a danger that the number of clergy leaving the parochial ministry for the social services or education would increase. "The pressure is growing and steps must be taken to reduce it."

These dangers arose from the changing world in which we lived. "But be of good cheer. The Lord has said 'I have overcome the world', and again, 'Against my Church the gates of hell shall not prevail'. Only 'watch and pray'. How better could the Bishop commend the people to God, "or you commend me, as I hope you do", than by making this memorial of our Lord's life, death, resurrection and ascension with its assurance of His continuing presence among us. "And this we are now about to do."

It was an inspiring address, showing clear insight into the deepest feelings of his clergy - they realised that Dr. Mortimer had understood their problems more than many had ever supposed.

After the service the Bishop and the Lord Lieutenant of Devon (Lord Roborough) stood by some microphones in the Nave of the Cathedral. Lord Roborough presented the Bishop with a cheque for £3,000 - a farewell gift from his people - after praising him for his great leadership in the Diocese. "During those years," Lord Roborough said, "there have been great changes, especially in the general moral outlook of this country. On all important issues the Bishop has spoken with great courage and wisdom. We would wish you to know what a tremendous help you have been to us." Referring to the Bishop's great contribution to the House of Lords debates, Lord Roborough added: "In some of the debates on moral issues you have been on the losing side, but we know very well that this did not mean you were on the wrong side."

The Bishop of Crediton then presented Dr. Mortimer with a gold watch inscribed "+ R.E. 1949-73" and in a witty speech referred to his 22 years as the Bishop's "stooge". By way of explanation Bishop Westall pointed out that in the Oxford Dictionary 'stooge' was defined as a deputy! The sad occasion drew to a rapid close with some final words from Bishop Mortimer.

At about this time the Bishop had some colour

photographs of himself taken and gave each of his clergy a choice of one out of two. One showed the Bishop in splendid episcopal robes with the Cathedral in the background, the other was of the Bishop in his study in lounge suit and purple stock. Dr. Mortimer did not look very well in these photographs; clearly he was feeling tired at the end of his 24 years' reign. Bishop Westall recalls that Dr. Mortimer said to him just after the Presentation, "Well, it's all finished." Bishop Westall added, "The thought crossed my mind that he felt his life was completed."

The time had arrived in September for the Bishop and Mrs. Mortimer to leave the Palace and move to their new home at the Old Rectory, Newton Reigny, a little village, three miles from Penrith in Cumbria. Bishop Westall noted that on this day the Bishop was particularly sad. The day before he had, quite suddenly and impulsively, decided to give nearly all his books to Exeter University Library. He simply rang up the Professor of Theology, Prof. J.R. Porter, and in a day or two the books were taken away.

The fact was that Dr. Mortimer was especially sad at having to live so far from Devon in retirement. It was not only that he had so many friends in Devon and had spent over a third of his life as Bishop of Exeter. He felt that he had natural connections with the Westcountry. His father had been born at Sidmouth, where he had spent many happy times. His brother Glanville had lived in retirement at nearby Seaton and his cousin Tom lived at Colyton, only two miles from the latter town. His family **belonged** to the West of England, too. It was at Dunster that his ancestor Mark had settled in 1510, and since then many of the family had lived in Devon, Somerset or Gloucestershire. His own childhood had been spent in Bristol and in Wiltshire. Cumbria was a beautiful county indeed, but it was too far from the parts that he knew and loved.

The Mortimers had never planned to live so far away. The Bishop had hoped to live in Devon or Somerset. But this was the time when house prices had hit the ceiling. Almost every house was being sold by auction and unbelievably high prices were being paid; between 1971 and 1973 houses generally had more than doubled in value. Unfortunately neither the central Church authorities nor the Diocese had secured a retirement house for the Bishop, and Dr. Mortimer himself had still made no definite arrangements about a house up to a few months before announcing his resignation.

The Bishop's requirements were not particularly ambitious, but he and Mrs. Mortimer naturally hoped to find a house about the size of a Rectory, especially as three of their family were married and frequently visited their parents, grandchildren and all! Also the Mortimers had a large circle of friends, many of whom they liked to have at their home from time to time. Houses of this kind fetched such high prices, however, that at the time they seemed to be almost beyond the Mortimers' reach. The Bishop very much wanted to live at Colyton, near his cousin, but when a suitable house came on the market he was unable to secure it at an auction. He was also interested in Upottery Vicarage which was for sale, but at the time the Church Commissioners, anxious to improve clergy stipends in the face of rampant inflation, were selling all unwanted vicarages by auction for very high sums.

In the end the problem was solved in an unexpected way. A lifelong friend of the Mortimers, who had lived for many years in Cumbria but was now living in retirement in the South of England, saw an advertisement for the Old Rectory at Newton Reigny in a magazine and sent the cutting to the Mortimers. At the time the Bishop was in the U.S.A.; his family consulted him about buying the house and this time were successful at the auction, so by the time the Bishop had returned from the States the house was theirs! The family were very relieved, even excited, at having obtained this pleasant residence. It was a typical 19th century rectory, in charming grey stone, near the middle of a pretty Lakeland village. Very close by was the nicely-kept 12th century church.

Robert Mortimer inevitably felt exiled in this distant retreat. He tried to make the best of it - at least it was a peaceful spot and he was relieved to have so much less strain on retirement. Dr. Thomas Bloomer, the retired Bishop of Carlisle, lived fairly near and the two bishops were good friends. Dr. Mortimer conducted services sometimes in various local churches and he celebrated Holy Communion regularly in the little village church. He often served at the altar there when the Vicar (Canon W.A. Batty, Vicar of Penrith) was celebrating; on the Bishop's death the Vicar expressed his gratitude for the quiet help given by his episcopal server. The *Carlisle Diocesan News* in November 1976 commented that Dr. Mortimer had been ready to help wherever needed in that Diocese and had always humbly put himself at the disposal of those who sought him out or invited him to address their Chapter or study group. He often visited Carlisle Cathedral and was well-known to the Dean and Chapter. He attended his successor's Enthronement in Exeter Cathedral on December 8th 1973, wearing lay dress and sitting amongst the congregation. He joined Penrith Cricket Club as a non-playing member and saw some of its matches.

On his retirement Dr. Mortimer was invited by the publishers Chatto and Windus to write an illustrated biography of St. Paul. He would like to have done this and the publishers offered him very favourable terms, but somehow he never got around to it. St. Paul was not one of his specialist fields, and although the firm offered to consider a subject of the Bishop's own choice, he never submitted one. Perhaps he was too tired at this stage to undertake a major new work.

Dr. Mortimer managed to travel up and down the country quite a lot during these last three years. He was pleased when the Bishop of Chichester asked him to be Chairman of a three-man Commission to consider the possibility of modifying the Rural Deanery boundaries in Chichester Diocese. The Commission was appointed in March 1975 and produced its Report the same year, less than twelve months before the Bishop's death. This involved two or three visits to Chichester.

Among the Bishop's papers was his engagement diary for 1976, the last year of his life. The main event that year was the Bishop's and Mrs. Mortimer's visit to the United States to stay with their daughter Sophia from June 27th-July 19th. This they did every other year, Sophia and her husband staying with them in the years in between. Robert seemed very well during this visit and was as delighted to see Sophia as she was to see him.

Every two months the Bishop attended a meeting of the Inter-Church Travel Advisory Committee and was actually booked to go on an Inter-Church cruise in November, two months after he died. From May 17th-20th he stayed in Devon with the Rector of Kenn (Rev. P.Mc. Crory) and attended the silver jubilee of the priesthood of the Rev. D.C. Vickery, Vicar of St. Peter's, Plymouth, which he much enjoyed. By May 28th the Bishop was in Oxford for Eights Week and doubtless another visit to his beloved Christ Church. On June 8th-9th he was at the Athenaeum, and on June 17th at Lord's. On June 19th he was back in Cumbria taking a church service; in another eight days, of course, he was off to the U.S.A. So although he often grumbled about his "exile" to Cumbria he was still doing much that was interesting. As late as April 2nd he had given his splendid lecture "Punishment in a Christian Society" to the Dyfed Branch of the Magistrates' Association at Aberystwyth. Sadly he was booked to attend the Apple Tree Dinner at Keble on September 29th, only a fortnight after his death.

Not recorded in the diary, strangely enough, was a visit which the Bishop made in March 1976 to stay with his old friend the Rev. Sir Patrick Ferguson-Davie who had lately sold his Crediton estate and gone to Cyprus to live. Sir Patrick noticed that Robert was in good form and very relaxed on this occasion. He had fallen in love with Cyprus and on his return home wrote to Sir Patrick that like the Queen of Sheba on Solomon "the half had not been told me." But in Cyprus the Bishop's leg had begun to give him trouble. While he was on the island his son Edward had flown in to visit him. Edward was not allowed to enter the Turkish part of Cyprus where Sir Patrick and Lady Ferguson-Davie lived, however, so at the end of his stay there the Bishop went with Sir Patrick's son to Limassol on the Greek side of the island for a few days to be with Edward. Sir Patrick's son was fascinated to hear the two Mortimers talking and reciting in Classical Greek as they walked around the sites at Paphos and Curium!

If the Bishop had at first felt lonely in Cumbria, he warmed to it towards the end of the three years. Visiting his friend Preb. G.H. Samuel at Paignton during his last stay in Devon in May 1976, Dr. Mortimer told him that he would be glad to get back to Newton Reigny as it was so much quieter there! His leg had given continuous trouble since his return from Cyprus; he told Prebendary Samuel that he could not now walk properly; ever since his holiday in Cyprus his gait had been unbalanced.

Returning to Cumbria in very good spirits after seeing his daughter, the Bishop spent August quietly, for the most part at home. At the beginning of September, however, he began to feel seriously unwell and thought that he was suffering from some complaint of the digestive tract. He did not see his doctor, though, for he was planning to motor to the Westcountry for ten days on September 11th and at the end of this trip he had arranged to take back an old friend from Bristol, who was going to stay for a week or two with the Mortimers at Newton Reigny. His idea had been to stay the night of September 11th with Mr. Arthur Derrick, who had played hockey for Somerset with him fifty years before. He was then going to spend a few days with Prebendary Souttar at Sidmouth Vicarage and make one or two other calls before driving back from Bristol with the friend.

On September 8th each year (the Nativity of the Blessed Virgin Mary) the Bishop and Mrs. Mortimer used to have a little celebration, since it was on this day in 1931 when the couple had had their first outing together in Austria. This year they could not manage it on September 8th, so it was on the 9th that they went to Hawes Water together and enjoyed lunch at a pleasant hotel at Bampton nearby. On September 10th the Bishop and his wife went to Penrith to do some shopping. Robert had had several bad nights before this but he seemed reasonably well on the shopping expedition.

On Saturday morning, September 11th, the Bishop said that he had had a good night but he had a nasty fall getting into the bath. This fall shook him and he decided that he could not motor to Bristol that day after all. Robert asked his wife if she would ring the doctor and she agreed, for he did not look at all well. She waited a few minutes until about 9 a.m., however, before going up to the bedroom again to ask her husband what to tell the doctor. When she got to the bedroom she found Robert lying on the floor. He had died suddenly from a ruptured aortic aneurysm - his wife had heard no sound from him during those minutes when she was downstairs preparing the breakfast. Strangely enough, Robert's father, though suffering from a different complaint, died in a very similar manner - the family had gone upstairs to find Edward Mortimer dead in the bedroom.

The Bishop was cremated privately at Carlisle on September 17th, no one attending this service. The ashes were taken to Newton Reigny Church, where Canon Batty conducted the funeral the next day. Many from the village attended the service, which was a quiet and dignified ceremony according to the Series 3 rite. Afterwards the casket containing Dr. Mortimer's ashes remained in the little church until taken to Exeter Cathedral. A Requiem Mass was sung at nearby Greystoke Church. In the latter parish a preliminary training course for intending ordinands is run at the Rectory, on which Mrs. Mortimer still gives her services as a teacher. The Requiem was accompanied by a nice choir and the ancient Contakion was sung.

On September 22nd a Requiem Mass was sung at Exeter Cathedral. The celebrant was Dr. Mortimer's successor, the Rt. Rev. E.A.J. Mercer, assisted by the Bishops of Crediton and Plymouth. The packed congregation included Mrs. Mortimer and some twenty family mourners, Sir Godwin Michelmore representing the Lord Lieutenant of Devon, the Mayor and Mayoress of Exeter, the High Sheriff of Devon, Viscountess Sidmouth, the Abbot of Buckfast, the Archdeacon of Oxford representing Christ Church, the Vice-Chancellor of Exeter University, the Warden of St. Edward's, Oxford, representatives of Keble College and the Woodard Corporation and the Bishop's faithful chauffeur, Mr. A.J. Chandler.

The address at the service was given by the Bishop's long-standing friend the Bishop of Crediton, Dr. W.A.E. Westall, who spoke with his accustomed warmth and perceptiveness. After the Eucharist the Bishop's ashes were laid to rest in his beloved St. Gabriel's Chapel, the committal being conducted by Canon F.G. Rice,

Dr. Mortimer's personal Chaplain for seventeen years. The Memorial Stone, designed by Mary Langhorne at Mrs. Mortimer's request, carries the inscription:
   + Robertus Episcopus Exoniensis 1949-73
   Uno pane vivunt cives utriusque patriae

On November 13th a Memorial Service for Dr. Mortimer was held at Christ Church Cathedral, Oxford. This was particularly appropriate, since not only had the Bishop been on the academic staff of the House for twenty years, and a Canon of the Cathedral for the last five of them, but his affection for the college was very great indeed. The Dean of Christ Church wrote to Mrs. Mortimer at the time: "I do not need to tell you in what deep affection and regard he was held here, and how warmly everyone looked forward to his visits to the House. He was a person one always hoped to be near in the Common Room. I first came to the House after he had moved to Exeter, and never had the luck to be his immediate colleague, but his kindnesses were immeasurable."

The service at Christ Church was attended by a distinguished gathering which included Archbishop Lord Ramsey and Lady Ramsey, Lady Fisher of Lambeth, Lord and Lady Blake, the Bishop of Chichester, Bishop H.J. Carpenter, Sir Kenneth Wheare, the Heads of several Oxford Colleges and the Chairman and Warden of St. Edward's, Oxford. The Dean of Christ Church conducted the service, the Warden of Keble read the Lesson and the Bishop of Oxford gave the Blessing. The address was given by Professor Gordon Dunstan of King's College, London; this was a brilliant piece of oratory which summed up the Bishop's contribution to English life as Bishop and scholar, Parliamentarian and member of high-level Committees.

"A light has gone out in the Church of England, for his magisterial presence, wise and learned counsel and lucid skill in debate are no longer available, save in the modified form of his literary works. The Diocese generally mourns the passing of an outstanding and distinguished leader, and a Father-in-God who gained universal respect; and many of us have lost a loyal friend of deep understanding and unwavering constancy. But in the context of faith and hope, our tears should be few and mostly hidden, for they should give place to praise and thanksgiving to God for the life and work of a great theologian and pastor, whom we were privileged to have as our Bishop for 24 years." These were the words of the Bishop's Chaplain, Canon F.G. Rice, in an article written shortly after the Bishop's death. True as was this description, once again not everyone would have seen Dr. Mortimer quite in this light. To many who did not know him well, he seemed rather remote and enigmatic as a person, though even to them the Bishop's monumental learning must have shone clearly through this disguise. His shy manner could never obscure his greatness.

Commenting in 1973 on the Bishop's coming retirement, *The Times* noted: "Dr. Mortimer, aged 70, was once strongly tipped to become Archbishop of Canterbury." Anyone who moved in the Bishop's circle will know how very widely, in fact, this view was held. More than one eminent ecclesiastic who wrote to the family on Dr. Mortimer's death observed that, unaccountably, the Bishop had not gained the promotion which he deserved. Yet strangely enough Dr. Mortimer told the writer and others shortly before his death that his one great ambition had been to become Dean of Christ Church, the college and Cathedral which had meant so much to him over the years.

No-one can fully plumb the depth of senior Crown appointments and it is common knowledge that the highest office rarely descends on the shoulders of those who deserve it most. However the real reason why Dr. Mortimer remained at Exeter many have been that he was able to make his greatest contribution to Church and State, to the glory of God and the well-being of his people, by remaining in the office which he held. Had the Bishop been appointed to Canterbury the great weight of extra meetings involved, the pressure of administration, the need for time-consuming world tours, would almost certainly have prevented him from doing what he did. His wise counsel in the House of Lords for so many years, his great contribution to Canon Law revision (the benefits of which may be felt for a century or more), his splendid services to Public School education, his unique care for the Religious Communities and his substantial contributions to prison reform would never have been given to the Church and nation. It is probable that when history has had time to tell its tale Dr. Mortimer may be more remembered than a number of Archbishops of Canterbury. We cannot do better than quote some words written by a noted Archbishop of Canterbury, Michael Ramsey, to Bishop Mortimer's Chaplain: "So a great and wonderful life on earth has ended. I shall for all my days remember him as a great bishop and a lovely, unique man."

THE END

ROBERT CECIL MORTIMER
Bishop of Exeter 1949-1973
Sermon preached by the Rev. Professor G.R. Dunstan at the Memorial Service, Christ Church Cathedral, Oxford, 12 November, 1976.

From *Ecclesiasticus.* 44:16 (or so it is said):
Behold a great priest, who in his days
pleased God and was found righteous.

From memories stored in a liturgically unregenerate youth - when the Church service was more encrusted with symbolism than is in favour now - from the Common (as I recall it) of a Confessor Bishop, words long forgotten now re-invest the mind, restored to tenancy there in these days of mourning for ROBERT CECIL MORTIMER, once a Student of this House, Regius Professor of Moral and Pastoral Theology in this University, then Bishop of Exeter and a Prelate and Peer of this Realm:
Behold a great priest, who in his days
pleased God and was found righteous.

The words are not, in fact, in Scripture as they are found in the Missal. For that Epistle for a Confessor Bishop a *catena* was made up, it would appear, from the Son of Sirach's praises of a line of men - Enoch, Noah, Abraham, Jacob, Aaron. So we have a portrait, not of one great priest, but of great priesthood. And it lay dormant in one mind until awakened by the obsequies of these last two months, quickened by the features of a man, a friend.

Presiding from Grandisson's lofty throne in his cathedral church of Exeter, surrounded by visible tokens, in scratched marble and alabaster, of Leofric, Henry Marshall, Simon of Apulia; Bronscombe the builder, Quivil the giver of the Constitutions; Stapeldon, Stafford; Lacy the scholar, pastor, healer - and how much he was at home in that company! - Robert Mortimer was a pontiff cast in an historic mould, the more memorable and the more endearing for being, perhaps, the last.

I

"Every High priest taken from among men is ordained in things pertaining to God, that he may offer both gifts and sacrifices for sins...."

It was as scholar first, and then as bishop, that he made his own the things pertaining to God, and offered them. This is no time to rehearse the story of his life, no time for the anecdotes we all could tell - and anecdotes cling to such a character, as rugged and deep-chiselled as the mollusc-covered North Devon rocks. Today we recall only those gifts to us left at each stage of his ministry.

Ruefully we reflect, sometimes, upon the unlawful embrace in which moral theology has been held by canon law. Mortimer's first appointment in this University was to a Lectureship in Early Canon Law. His study in that discipline was deep. It gave us his first major book, *The Origins of Private Penance in the Western Church* (1939) - a work whose fine distinctions have yet to take root in the less tutored of clerical minds, even more in popular imagination. As a canonist, too, he saved from extinction, and re-clothed with competence, the tenuous tradition of a clerical Diocesan Chancellor. As such, too, he gave to the Archbishops' Commission on Canon Law, a fund of knowledge and a practical judgement which made the Report of that Commission (1947) more than a piece of historical scholarship, admirably written, more by far than a Committee draft for Church reform. Grounded in authentic canonical tradition (with its strong theological, moral and juridical roots) the Report stands as a monument to a vision of what the Church of England historically was and might still have been; a vision shared by that remarkable band of scholars and divines among whom Mortimer found his place - Selwyn, Vaisey, Claude Jenkins, Ernest Jacob, and Hamilton Thompson to whom I was once as a child.

In the twenty years which followed he worked again, to try to hold the Convocations and the Church Assembly to the entirety and the integrity of that vision.

His later book, *Western Canon Law* (1953), was written while he was busy with that attempt. Its later chapters contain his judgements of what remains of the old canon law in the government and discipline of the Church, what called still for reform, and the dangers and difficulties attending reform. The lectures established his reputation in the United States of America; they are profitable reading for students and ordinands still.

There was in him, of course, a marriage of learning with temperament. As a man he was equipped to rule; as a bishop, so formed, he knew how to rule. For him the pastoral staff had its true significance: the symbol of canonical authority. What has sentimentality done to the Twenty-third Psalm, with soft melodies? "The Lord is my shepherd," we say. He knew it as in the Vulgate: *"Dominus regit me"*. And, as a shepherd, he ruled. Not for him the model of a Bishop as the chief executive of a standing committee. Not for him, either, a Church polity which compounds an enfeebled democracy with an enfranchised bureaucracy. For him words kept their meaning. A synod was a bishop in council, first of all; with whom he took council was open to discussion.

II

His study of the canon law, then, taught him how to rule. The purpose and destination of that rule the law could not teach: that came from moral theology - God's lore for shepherds with flocks in charge. This gift, too, he made his own, and offered.

Its first monument was written while he was here, and Regius Professor in the University. It was *The Elements of Moral Theology* (1947), dedicated to Kenneth Kirk, once his predecessor in his Chair, then Bishop of Oxford - his friend and teacher (and - if I may say so - and mine). (So runs a tradition: who has not felt it, in affection, admiration, and sheer debt, running in his veins?)

The theses on Kirk are beginning to be written; soon they will begin on Mortimer also; and we must leave to them the comparison of the first edition of that book with the second, revised. The book is systematic in a now almost forgotten sense. It begins with the shepherd's destination - "The End of Man" in the vision and glory of

God. It studies Law in its several parts, as Hooker and Aquinas studied it; then Human Action and the Morality of Acts; last, the Virtues, all seven, and each set in its logical place in the total scheme, and in its quickening place in human experience.

Here, reading the book again after many years, we see Jacob and the angel, wrestling: Mortimer obedient to an intellectual tradition wrestling with Mortimer himself intellectually aware and humanly driven to develop that tradition - to keep tradition as what it truly is, a living, organic power in the theological and spiritual life of the Church and of men. Thus, on page 8 he can write that "the whole of creation is under the governance of God, Who works out in it His purpose. That purpose is the Eternal Law." But by page 14 he is already pleading "the need today for fresh, hard thinking on the application of the natural law to new conditions and circumstances, and for effort to elucidate its content" - a plea which he repeated in the Church Assembly in July 1963, adding that the study should now be done with the assured conclusions of modern psychology in view. And those conclusions would surely call in question God's assured governance in the created order.

The structure of his book, and of his exposition in every part of it, he owed to Aquinas. Yet the direction of his exposition - that to which it tends - he owed to experience, observation, and a ripening wisdom of his own. His illustrations, too, come from two minds - the Angel's mind (if you like) and plain Jacob's. The Angel's are ecclesiastical, and dated, like the obligation to fast before Communion, assumed, unargued; or the conscience tortured by the thought of an "inter-denominational service" without leave of the Bishop. Jacob's come from common neighbourliness, like the obligation to assure that the wind will not carry the smoke into your neighbour's window before you light your autumn bonfire; and from the hard decisions which doctors face, or statesmen, or men of war.

It was this skill in practical moral reasoning which he developed most in his later years - when the Oxford moralist had become, not Bishop of Exeter only, but a Bishop in the Church of England also and a Peer of the

Realm.

Not the printed word, in great measure, but personal observation is the chief authority here - the observation of one who, holding a minor office in Church House, had to listen, and to chase ideas, and to pass a paper around for comment, and to draw men together and set them talking, and make something of their words. It was Robert Mortimer who, addressing the British Medical Association in Torquay in 1960, launched a discussion which still does not flag on the doctor's duty not to kill, but not to strive officiously to keep us alive. And when, sixteen years later, I pick up an article from a medical journal from somewhere in America which begins to discuss the determination of death with King Lear holding his looking glass to Cordelia, I know what the author has been cribbing (1): it is from one of those pamphlets which came from Church House in those years, when Mortimer was either smoking his way through the problems with us, or writing cryptic comments from Exeter to help us along.

His restatement of *retribution* as an essential ingredient in punishment - a merciful restraint upon vengeance and upon all punitive abuse of power - wrung out of him as a member of the Advisory Committee on the Penal System, was a model of what essential re-statement should always be (2). And one debt the nation owes to him in chief; that is a Divorce Law free from its ancient and hypocritical encumbrance of the matrimonial offence - the necessity for a petitioner to prove himself innocent and his partner guilty in order to secure matrimonial relief: an unchristian exercise, surely, to prove oneself innocent and the other guilty, yet one which - but for the advocacy of Mortimer, and the enormous moral authority attaching to his word, the Church of England would have fought for in 1967 as it had fought for it for over half a century before. He it was who chaired the Archbishop's Commission which produced *Putting Asunder* (1966); he it was who recalled the House of Lords to the essence of the matter, in a short brilliant speech, when the shutters of tedium were closing in; he it was who, alone, negotiated that compromise between the Church and the Law Commission which enabled the present statute to be enacted. and the law to

1. *Decisions about Life and Death*, Church Information Office, 1965.
2. *Crucible*, Church Information Office, January, 1963.

emerge the cleaner - though the problem of divorce still looms (3). Such was the gift of the moralist to his Church and nation.

III

If, then, these were the gifts of Mortimer the canonist and moral theologian, it was supremely on the altar of his diocese that he offered them to God. His ministry there is recorded - on paper, certainly, in the analytical notes which he wrote, month by month, in the *Exeter Diocesan Leaflet*, on problems great and small of Church and Nation. But more they are recorded in the affections of the clergy and people of every corner of Devon. And not in their affections only, but in their lives, ordained and lay.

He was a moral and intellectual force, respected everywhere, sometimes rather feared; sparing in its application to what the academic world (God forgive it!) calls serious work, but unsparing in its ministry to the needs of his clergy and people. From the Palace into which he fitted as by nature formed - with the arms of Courtenay carved in the mantel stone, telling successive generations of the twin guardians of God's people there, bishop and earl - from there he went out, by day and night, to serve. When affection flashed out of him, from behind the reticent mask, it won deep affection in return. And always men knew that he stood for them *pros ton Theon* "on the Godward side".

IV

It is further written of the priest in *Hebrews* that "he can have compassion on the ignorant, and on them that are out of the way, for that he himself also is compassed with infirmity."

Robert Mortimer's compassion runs through all his writing; and it was evident in his judgements upon men, on the reality of their problems, their struggles and temptations. He knew his own infirmities. His friends, his clergy and his people knew them too. Half the anecdotes they tell about him would have no point were they not

3. *Theology, LXXIV, 1971, p 123f; cf p.1.*

about a man, a real man, who knew what he couldn't do - boredoms, provocations he could not endure. As a canonist he knew the canonical law, that a priest must be without physical blemish, as the lamb was, for on the altar of God he must first lay himself.

As a moralist he knew the unswerving law by which God has bound Himself, that there is no sin which God's mercy will not forgive, and from which God's grace will not deliver any man in whom is that desire.

He lived in that knowledge, and by that desire, for forgiveness, mercy, grace.

As a simple believer in Christ he knew what true priesthood was, and where, he had an Advocate with the Father, to whom he lifted up, not his heart only, but his office, his bishopric, as well.